DORKING'S RAILWAYS

by

Alan A. Jackson

DORKING LOCAL HISTORY GROUP
1988

First published in 1988 by the Local History Group of the Dorking and District Preservation Society, Dorking Museum, West Street, Dorking, Surrey RH4 1BS.

ISBN 1 870912 01 2

Printed by Rayment Printers Ltd., 5 Horsham Road, Dorking, Surrey.

Cover picture: Up passenger train leaving Box Hill (SE&CR) for Redhill c. 1905. The bridge over the LBSCR line is at the extreme right. Box Hill is in the background; the foreground area is now the end of Deepdene Avenue Road and Deepdene Vale, housing built in the 1920s and 1930s for commuters on the former LBSCR line. (From a postcard by G. W. Smith, Dorking.)

Preface and Acknowledgements

Fifty years ago, in North London, a Fifth Form schoolboy pored over a one inch to the mile Ordnance Survey map of the Dorking area, trying to answer a list of questions he was asked to attempt after studying the features portrayed. Prominent on the map, running north to south, and east to west, were the railways. These exercised a profound fascination, then and ever since, and questions about them were answered enthusiastically. Nine years later, Dorking was visited for the first time, on a demobilisation train working between Dover and Rugeley, but it was near midnight, and after four years away from England, sleeping in fits and starts, the war-weary traveller was too excited at the prospect of freedom to care about where he was, or even to remember that geography examination map.

Later it was discovered what a pleasant place Dorking was, splendidly set amongst the gentle, largely unspoiled Surrey Hills, retaining much of its relaxing country town ambience. In an age when much of the country's railway system was being destroyed, sometimes quite unwisely, on often dubious premises, it was particularly pleasing to realise that the town had managed to defy Beeching and those of like mind, emerging from that dark period with virtually all the railway facilities it had ever had, including all four stations, though sadly, with one notable exception, the charming Victorian buildings were first neglected, then demolished. Eventually, deciding there was no better place to spend retirement than in this fortunate spot, a suitable house was acquired within the distant and friendly sound of both lines. Those railways, first seen on a school desk half a century before, were now found to deserve closer study.

Hence this little book. I hope it will encourage Dorkinians to value and use their railway heritage, stoutly defending it against any future threats and that it may also stimulate others to explore this lovely district by train and on foot.

I am most grateful to all who have helped with information and anecdotes, particularly that meticulous recorder of local railway artefacts and former Southern Railwayman, John Harrod, of Warnham, and former LBSCR and SR Dorking railwayman Charles Wiscombe. There are many others who should be thanked, among them Klaus Marx, archivist of the Bluebell Railway Preservation Society for supplying photographs and locomotive information; Bob Padgham of Dorking for finding me a copy of Henry Thomas Hope's agreement regarding the passage of the railway through the Deepdene Estate; Mary Sutton for pointing me to an important and elusive date; Mary, Vivien Ettlinger and other fellow committee members of the Dorking Local History Group for encouragement and support ever since the book was first planned; H. V. Borley and John Faulkner of the Railway Club for

3

reading and commenting on early drafts; Lionel Green of Dorking for the same chore and many helpful suggestions; Miss E. Clear of the Dorking & District Museum for guiding me through the extensive records in the Upper Room; and Beryl Higgins for expertly converting my rough maps and plans to presentable form. My longtime friend, Dr. Edwin Course, of Southampton University, very kindly made available a proof copy of his introduction to the Surrey Record Society's valuable publication on the Reading, Guildford & Reigate Railway (SRS Volume XXXIII, 1987) as well as his personal notes on the Reigate-Guildford line.

Finally I should perhaps make it clear that the boundaries of 'Dorking' for the purposes of this book are broadly those of the former Urban District. This explains the omission of any detailed account of Holmwood station and of any reference to the Dorking Greystone Lime Company's system near Betchworth station. For the first I would refer those interested to part 7 of John Harrod's article *Up the Dorking* (see bibliography) and for the second, to J. L. Townsend's excellent little book, *Townsend Hook and the Railways of The Dorking Greystone Lime Co. Ltd.*, published by the Brockham Museum Association in 1980.

ALAN A. JACKSON
Dorking, July 1988.

ABBREVIATIONS

BR	British Railways
GWR	Great Western Railway (BR Western Region from 1 January 1948)
HDLR	Horsham Dorking & Leatherhead Railway
LBSCR	London Brighton & South Coast Railway (SR from 1 January 1923)
LSWR	London & South Western Railway (SR from 1 January 1923)
m	miles
RG&RR	Reading, Guildford & Reigate Railway
SER	South Eastern Railway (SR from 1 January 1923)
SR	Southern Railway (BR Southern Region from 1 January 1948)

CONTENTS

MAPS AND PLANS

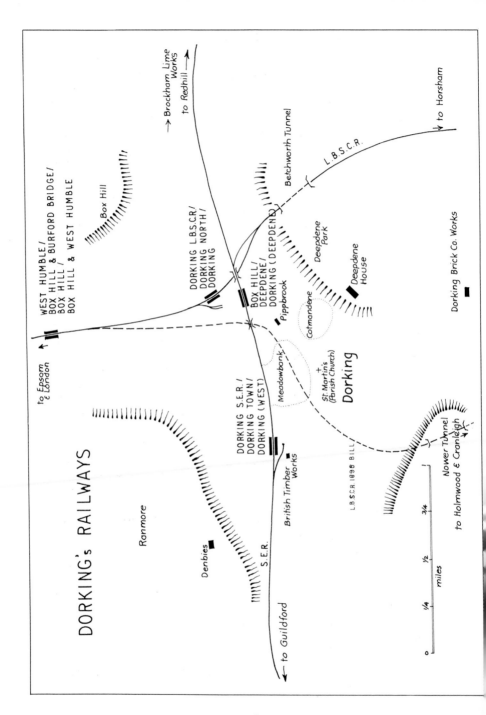

DORKING's RAILWAYS

WEST HUMBLE /
BOX HILL & BURFORD BRIDGE /
BOX HILL /
BOX HILL & WEST HUMBLE

Box Hill

→ Brockham Lime Works
to Redhill →

to Epsom
& London

DORKING L.B.S.C.R /
DORKING NORTH /
DORKING

BOX HILL /
DEEPDENE /
DORKING (DEEPDENE)

Pippbrook

Cotmandene

Betchworth Tunnel

Deepdene Park

Deepdene House

L.B.S.C.R.

to Horsham

Ranmore

Denbies

S.E.R.

British Timber Works

DORKING S.E.R. /
DORKING TOWN /
DORKING (WEST)

Meadowbank

St. Martin's
(Parish Church)

Dorking

Dorking Brick Co. Works

L.B.S.C.R 1898 BILL

Nower Tunnel
to Holmwood & Cranleigh

to Guildford

0   ¼   ½   ¾
miles

6

Dorking's First Railway

On the map of Dorking the railways form a slightly distorted cross, following as they do the valleys of the Pippbrook and the Mole east and west and the Mickleham Gap through the North Downs north to south. These natural corridors attracted the engineers of several early and aborted schemes, notably some of the first proposals to connect London and Brighton, and also the Direct London & Portsmouth Railway, authorised by parliament in 1846 and planned to run from the Croydon and Epsom Railway at Epsom through Dorking and Gomshall and thence to Godalming, Havant and Portsmouth[1].

Both the South Eastern and the London, Brighton & South Coast Railways deposited bills in the 1845-6 session for a branch line from Redhill to Dorking but these were overtaken by the first successful project affecting the town. This was the independently-promoted Reading, Guildford & Reigate Railway (RG&RR), a 46½ mile line sanctioned by Acts of 1846 and 1847[2]. Child of a syndicate of London and Surrey businessmen and bankers (none from Dorking), its stated objective was to secure through traffic passing between the west, north and midlands and the Channel ports, avoiding the congestion in London and thus saving time, distance and expense. Any benefit given to intermediate points between Reading and Redhill, such as Dorking, would be incidental. At the time (1841 census) Dorking town had a mere 3,400 inhabitants and there were only some 11,000 in the catchment area. Nevertheless, the proprietor of Castle Mill told the parliamentary committee that he would use the railway to bring red wheat from Reading to mix with the local white, whilst R. W. Phelps, owner of Dorking Waterworks, perceptively suggested the potential for tourist traffic, a subject we shall refer to later.

Between Dorking and Gomshall, the RG&RR took the alignment surveyed for the Direct London & Portsmouth Railway, which scheme had effectively been abandoned as a through route by mid-1848, when the RG&RR was under construction. The South Eastern Railway (SER), which had a station at Redhill (then called Reigate Road) on its main London Bridge to Dover line, took an interest in the RG&RR from an early stage, securing two seats on the board for its own directors and eventually consenting to lease and work the new railway, which would be connected to its Tonbridge and Dover line at Redhill. In this way the SER was to secure a deep penetration into territory so far staked out by the London & South Western (LSWR) and Great Western (GWR). Parliament sanctioned these arrangements, also giving the SER an option to purchase the Redhill to Dorking section.

Little difficulty was encountered in securing the necessary land but by threatening to oppose the railway in parliament, Henry Thomas Hope of Deepdene, who owned most of the required strip to the east of the

7

town, exacted the inflated price of £300 an acre in contrast to the £160 an acre paid to William John Evelyn for similar property west of Dorking. The contractor for the Redhill to Dorking section was the Reigate-based George Wythes, whose contract was dated 25 June 1847. He performed well, completing the works to time. Between Dorking and Shalford Junction, construction was undertaken by Charles Henfrey, to a contract dated 29 May 1848. Some of the construction materials, including larchwood sleepers and rails, were delivered by road to Dorking, presumably via Redhill station. The initial engineering was in the hands of Francis Giles, with Robert Stephenson as consulting engineer, the latter taking over for a few months after Giles' death in March 1847, but not making any significant changes. Finally, from later in 1847, completion of the project fell to the SER's consulting engineer, Peter Barlow.

With seven trains daily provided by the SER into what is now Dorking West station, and six departures, the line from that point to Redhill was opened on 4 July 1849. There were intermediate stations at Betchworth and Reigate Town. None of the buildings was ready for that day and temporary arrangements had to be made. Through working between Redhill ('Reigate Junction') and Reading was established on 15 October the same year, the delay caused by engineering problems with the two LSWR tunnels south of Guildford station and the doubts of the Railway Inspecting Officer regarding an underline road bridge at Shere.

Three years later the SER purchased the RG&RR company, guaranteeing a five per cent dividend on its Ordinary Stock. This was rather more than the line was earning, but the SER feared that if it did not make an attractive offer others might step into its place.

Through Dorking the alignment of the double track was mostly below the scarp of the North Downs, on a route largely dictated by the physiography and the necessity of avoiding the existing built up area of the town. Westward of Betchworth this produced gradients of 1 in 116 and 1 in 215 down to the Mole crossing, which was approached on an embankment formed of spoil carried from the Brockham cutting half a mile to the west. Then, immediately beyond the five arch brick viaduct over the Mole, there began a four-mile climb along the base of the North Downs at 1 in 100 and 1 in 96 up to the RG&RR's summit, 1¼m east of Gomshall station where the line crossed the division of the catchment areas of the Mole and the Wey. In the days of steam, this long gradient created problems for heavy Down trains. Long, loose-coupled freights would sometimes divide from the stresses caused by stopping and re-starting at signals and heavy trains required banking assistance at the rear. To help with such difficulties, the SER soon split the five mile block section between Dorking and Gomshall, providing a small intermediate signal box called Westcott. This lonely outpost was on the Down or south side of the line immediately west of the underline bridge at Coomb Farm and 2m 143yd west of Dorking Station Box. It survived until 13 March

8

1935. Also on this gradient, catch points were placed 625 yards east of the Westcott box to derail any runaway vehicles on the Down line. When travelling in the Up (eastbound) direction, heavy freight trains have sometimes got out of control when descending incautiously. Thus on 21 November 1970 there was a spectacular derailment of an engineer's train at the Deepdene road bridge, some of the fifty–ton wagons spilling their ballast contents on to the A24, obstructing road traffic for a considerable time. A similar derailment occurred at Deepdene station on 25 January 1973, on that occasion involving a stone train.

Westcott Intermediate Signal Box and SER train for Reading, looking towards Dorking, c. 1880 (Photographer unknown).

There were three level crossings of bridle paths and farm roads in the Dorking district, each provided with a single storey cottage for the crossing-keeper and any family; all were on the north side of the railway. Coming from the east, the first was at Brockham (crossing no. 4) on the track up to the quarry and lime works. In September 1848 the inhabitants of Brockham had petitioned the RG&RR board for a station at this point but were denied that luxury. Milton (crossing no. 5) was sited west of Dorking station on the road to Milton Court chalkpit and lime kiln and Westcott (crossing no. 6) was at the point where Holehill Lane crossed the line. Apart from Milton, where there was a well on the south side of the line, these cottages received their water supply in cans delivered daily by train, a procedure which could still be observed in the late 1960s. Very soon after that time, Westcott and Milton crossings, by then almost devoid of any vehicular traffic, were left unmanned and these two bridle ways are now protected only by manual gates and notices. Looking at them today, it is apparent that those who lived in these two places must have led very lonely if tranquil lives, with the railway almost their only link with civilisation; in latter years, only a few farm workers and ramblers would need to cross the line through their gates. At Brockham, where there was some car traffic to and from cottages north of the line, automatic half barriers and flashing lights were installed in the 1970s. All three of the crossing-keeper's houses were demolished when these changes were made.

Westcott Crossing (Holehill Lane) looking to Dorking, 20 February 1965, 'Tadpole' diesel-electric set 1206 on Reading train approaching. Note drinking water cans by the crossing cottage. (Photo: Alan A. Jackson)

Brockham Crossing and cottage looking to Reigate, 'Tadpole' diesel-electric set 1202 on Reading train approaching, 29 July 1973. (Photo: Alan A. Jackson)

Understandably, the inhabitants of Dorking were anxious to have their station at the nearest point to the town. A memorial submitted to the RG&RR board in August 1846 had suggested a site on the east side of the church, opening from an area called 'The Lordships' (the present Meadowbank recreation ground). This would have been about midway between the present Dorking (Deepdene) and Dorking West Stations but since it was in a cutting, it would have been impossibly expensive to open it out for provision of freight facilities and even a simple passenger station, requiring a lengthy new access road, would have been unduly costly. Peter Barlow, the SER engineer, subsequently chose the level site at the west end of the cutting. Although this was half a mile north west of the market place and almost out of the town, Barlow comforted the directors by pointing out that this position was on a road leading to the district north of the line whilst being equally near the main population to the south; and it was also the most economical and suitable place for the construction of goods and passenger facilities. His recommendation was accepted in a move which did not please the good people of Dorking. With George Eives as their spokesman, 166 of them told the RG&RR board in March 1849 of their unqualified preference for a station near to and west of the London Road, at the point where the embankment changed to a cutting (i.e. immediately south of the west end of the present Croft Avenue), and requiring only a short approach road. Despite visits to the sites by the railway company's chairman and a meeting with the deputation at Dorking on 26 April 1849, the engineer's choice prevailed, although, as we shall see shortly, the protests of the townspeople were not entirely in vain.

For the new station, the company provided a building of some merit which looked well against the beautiful backdrop of Ranmore. It had two storeys, the upper one, with its steeply-pitched high gables, providing domestic accommodation for the stationmaster and his family. Gordon Biddle considers that Dorking was the best of all the RG&RR *cottage orné* stations, despite an excess of chimney stacks. 'Here', he writes, 'the restrained styling . . . in mellow brick relieved by exposed timbering and tiled roofs, fitted as perfectly into the Surrey Hills as any railway building could'[3]. A record of a payment to 'Mr. Wood, the architect's account' in the January 1850 minutes of the RG&RR suggests that Sancton Wood (1814-86) was the architect of the station at Dorking and the similar ones at Reigate, Betchworth, Chilworth and Shalford, although no doubt, as engineer at the crucial time, Peter Barlow had a considerable say in the overall design.

Freight facilities were eventually provided on both sides of the line, three roads on the south (Down) side serving a large goods shed and a coal wharf. Immediately adjacent, to the south, was the British Timber Works (Messrs. Brookers). By the early 1900s this was at its peak, employing about 100 men and with its several acres of stacking yards, was

11

Exterior of Dorking Town station, 30 March 1959. (Photo: J. N. Faulkner)

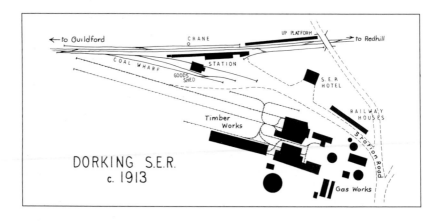

served by an internal narrow gauge rail layout (see Appendix). A little
to the east was the small Dorking Gas Works. Neither of these two
establishments was rail-connected at any stage despite their proximity
to the goods yard, a short-sighted economy which involved much costly
transhipment to and from road vehicles. On the north side, parallel with
the Up line, was a siding paid for by Thomas Cubitt when he was building
Denbies, his great mansion at the top of Ranmore, in 1850-1. This not
only served to bring in the initial building materials but subsequently
handled the traffic to and from this large estate. It was equipped with
its own cattle pens and eight-ton crane.

12

Dorking Town station looking towards Guildford c. 1903. (Photo: Dorking Museum)

There were crossovers at each end of the station layout, with a signal box at the west end of the Down platform. By the 1890s the station was able to handle all types of traffic, including transhipment of road vehicles. The small carriage dock provided for this purpose at the east end of the Down platform was used for unloading the elephants and other items for the circus which came to Cotmandene every year until World War 2.

Coal arrived at Dorking from Erith Wharf and later from the new East Kent pits to feed the retorts of the gasworks and the furnaces of the Dorking Brick Company at North Holmwood. Domestic fuel from collieries all over the country was delivered by rail for the several Dorking coal merchants. Other regular traffics here included groceries and provisions for Kingham & Company's warehouse in Station Road and huge tree trunks from the west country which the Timber Works would transform into various articles.

In 1848 John Belchambers of Dorking, who had provided a horse bus and coach connection to the SER station at Redhill since its opening applied for a lease of RG&RR railway land at the new station on which to erect an inn. Eventually railway travellers were served by a building in the station approach road which for many years was prominently labelled *The South Eastern Railway Hotel*. It still exists, now called *The Pilgrim*. In the early years, a horse bus met all trains to convey passengers to and from the town centre and standing for hire in the station forecourt were horse cabs, replaced by motor vehicles in the 1910s. The cabs were originally operated by Eleanor Holden of *The Red Lion*, Dorking, who sought in them some compensation for road trade lost after the opening of the line. She had told the RG&RR board in August 1848 that she and her family had been involved in 'posting etc.' at Dorking for upwards

13

of 30 years and there was no other person in the town in a position to do justice to the appointment as provider of cabs at the proposed station. The directors of the new railway, well aware of the value of roads and road traffic as feeders of the railway, agreed in 1848 to pay H. M. Parratt £25 towards the cost of a new road which he proposed to build over Ranmore Common to link the station directly to the Bookhams and Effingham. In more recent times, the cabs at the SER (later SR) station were owned and operated by Arthur King and later by Bill King, whose activities were based on stables at the SER Hotel. Nearby, in the station approach road, which was owned and maintained by the railway, the SER subsequently erected a terrace of small cottages to house railway staff.

As at some of the other stations on the RG&RR, Dorking's platforms were staggered, the Up one beginning opposite the eastern end of the Down. This feature, not uncommon in early railway stations, was supposed to make crossing of the line safer, since if there were two trains in the station at the same time, passengers would pass behind both. Irritation soon built up over the danger of walking over the railway from one platform to another and there was also concern about the considerable drop between the carriage steps and the low platforms. After several times complaining to the SER without result, the Dorking Local Board took the matter to the Board of Trade, a move which stimulated some action. In 1885 the SER undertook improvements to the passenger station which included construction of a subway between the two platforms.

Dorking Town station, Down platform, looking towards Guildford, 30 March 1959. (Photo: J. N. Faulkner)

Right through to the 1920s, what we now know as Dorking West was a station of some importance, although inevitably suffering loss of prestige and traffic once a more direct route to London had been opened by the LBSCR in 1867. After that it was for many years known informally in the town as 'Old Dorking'. Until the electrification of the shorter route in 1925/29 it remained popular with some commuters, since it provided direct access to the convenient City terminus of Cannon Street. In 1910 there were departures at 06.56, 07.28, 08.03, 08.25, 08.55 and 09.06, all of which would carry the businessman into Cannon Street in around one hour, and altogether there were about 20 trains each weekday to and from London Bridge or Cannon Street, some terminating at Dorking. One passenger facility found here until a relatively late date were the metal footwarmers which were placed in carriages not fitted with steam-heating pipes. This indicates that very old vehicles remained in use on this line for many years. It is recorded that as late as 1921 footwarmers were still sometimes to be seen at Dorking[4] and in his reminiscences of 60 years of life in the town written in 1950, E. L. Sellick also refers to this and another antiquated feature of the SER trains:

'The Dorking Town station was considered the premier station. Passengers who were prepared to tip the porter were able to secure footwarmers in cold weather and believe me, one was certainly wanted. I forget exactly which morning train it was between 8 and 9 a.m. but it stood in the Up Siding each night, and on being drawn into the platform on cold winter days the windows were covered with ice . . . [the footwarmers] were metal cylinders approximately 2 feet 6 by 9 inches filled with hot water heated in a boiler on the platform. The boiler was capable of holding about two dozen footwarmers at a time and was installed on the London platform. It was heated by a small furnace which had a stovepipe some 8 or 9 feet in height and the whole apparatus closely resembled Stephenson's 'Rocket'. The first lighting I remember was by oil lamps and the porters were obliged to run along the roofs of the carriages in order to ignite the burners by means of a taper.'[5]

Although the name Dorking Town given by the Southern Railway (SR) in July 1923 was somewhat misleading, it persisted until BR more accurately adopted Dorking West on 11 May 1987. With the formation of the SR in 1923, services, staff and accounts at the three stations in Dorking were gradually rationalised. Around 1930, the goods and mineral accounts were amalgamated with those at the former LBSCR station and the passenger traffic slowly declined (that to London had all but disappeared by World War 1). By 1933 stationmaster E. E. G. Blackman was responsible not only for Dorking Town, but Dorking North, Deepdene and Boxhill.

Freight services also fell away in the 1930s as road vehicles secured a major share, although the railway retained its staple business in solid fuels and building materials, as well as some lucrative sundries such as the longstanding contract with Woolworths. Following a brief revival in World War 2 when road transport suffered from petrol, diesel and other shortages, the decline steepened sharply, with road securing most of the remaining business in towns such as Dorking. Immediately after World War 1 there were 17 men at Dorking Town station, but by 1957 only six remained. That year saw the retirement of 'Sunshine Jack', a porter so-named because he greeted every train with the cry 'Dorking for Sunshine'.

With revenue from freight in seemingly terminal decline, Beeching's accountants decreed closure of the goods yard, and this took place on 6 May 1963. The signal box survived until the autumn of the following year, when the rails in the goods yard were finally removed. Further staff reductions took place around this time and manning at the station became patchy. Ageing gas lamps were neglected and building maintenance was ignored. No-one lived over the shop any more and in its somewhat isolated situation on the very edge of the town, the station became an unpleasant place to use at night. A report in the local paper in 1966[6] recounted the experiences of a 17-year old girl arriving at Dorking Town by train after dark. When the exceptionally long drop from the carriage to the 'practically unlit' platform (something the SER evidently had not corrected in 1885) caused the young lady to trip, 'there was not a soul of any description in sight' to assist her. Getting herself up, she then found what appeared to be the way out but the door was firmly locked. The darkness and silence worried her, as with mounting panic, she tried other doors without success. Eventually she discovered a narrow passage which led her to the forecourt, where she managed to read a notice explaining that owing to shortage of staff the ticket office had closed. Two gravel paths offered no indication whence they led and there was no-one to ask. Somehow she found the way, reaching Station Road thoroughly upset, feeling as if she had taken part in 'one of those television thrillers where all signs of life in a normally busy place had suddenly and unaccountably disappeared'. She could not face returning the same way later that evening.

Some of these problems were drastically removed in December 1969 when the pleasant but now much decayed station building was razed to the ground, to be replaced by tiny glass and steel bus-stop type shelters, brilliant fluorescent lighting on tall posts and some oak seats. Within a week young vandals had done their best to wreck much of these new features.

Today only the staggered platforms, the subway, the hotel, the goods shed and the terrace of railway houses remain to remind the visitor of what was for almost 20 years Dorking's main station and the hub of its railway activities. It is many years since the track ganger and his men could be seen sweeping the approach road each Saturday morning. Their care is replaced by a mess of litter and potholes. Direction signs installed by BR have long since fallen to the attentions of young vandals or become obscured by trees. It takes a determined traveller with a good sense of direction to find the unstaffed platforms, well hidden amidst junk yards, garages and workshops. Regulars and Dorkinians do of course know the way and surprisingly passengers are still to be seen at this inhospitable place, now the least-used of the three Dorking stations. Loss of its regular hourly service and Sunday trains in 1986 has only added to the pace of its decline and its future may not be assured.

A Second Station

The dissatisfaction of the town with the siting of the RG&RR station has already been mentioned. Whilst the original directors were unmoved, the SER, no doubt with its eye on the threat of another line coming south through the Mickleham Gap, evidently thought something more than the outpost in the far north west corner of the town was justified. On 7 September 1850 a local newspaper announced:

'. . . a platform is now in course of erection on the South Eastern Railway close to Mr. Alexander Robertson's nursery garden on the London Road, for the accommodation of the public at Mickleham, Leatherhead etc. It is intended by the Company to run an omnibus to and from those places for the convenience of passengers, free of expense.'[7]

This station, three quarters of a mile east of the first, was opened early in 1851, first appearing in Bradshaw's timetable in February under the name 'Box Hill and Leatherhead Road'. The suggestion that it served Leatherhead was quickly dropped, possibly because the proposed bus service did not endure, or even appear. In March 1851 it became simply 'Box Hill' but from 9 July 1923 the SR chose 'Deepdene' to avoid confusion with the station at West Humble, which was closer to the hill. BR changed it to the more helpful 'Dorking (Deepdene)' on 11 May 1987, an occasion which the local Rotary Club celebrated by donating a metal seat for the Up platform.

Erected on the embankment leading to the Mole Viaduct and immediately east of the London Road, this new station was restricted to passenger traffic and constructed as cheaply as possible. There were just two simple timber side platforms, the Up one served by a wooden building housing a ticket office, waiting and porters' rooms and lavatories, the Down with a small canopied wooden waiting shelter. Wooden stairways on each side of the embankment, affording access from the main road, were protected by curved corrugated iron roofs. Passengers entered on the north side and after passing through the ticket hall, those proceeding in the Guildford direction crossed the tracks under the supervision of the staff. No footbridge or subway was ever provided. A signal box at the Reigate end of the Up platform controlled the crossover nearby and the junction to the LBSCR, which will be mentioned later, but both box and crossover disappeared in the early 1920s. The stationmaster occupied a small house by the Pipp Brook, close to the town side of the embankment.

Box Hill Station SER (now Dorking (Deepdene)) looking towards Reigate c. 1905. The stationmaster and his dog, a ticket collector and two porters are ready to greet the Up train which is signalled. Box Hill in the background. (From a commercial postcard)

Shortly after its opening, the station was patronised by the Prince Consort, Queen Victoria's husband. He alighted here on 15 July 1851, proceeding via the new carriage drive from the Leatherhead Road to inspect Cubitt's recently−completed house and grounds on Ranmore, returning later that day from the main SER station. With the construction of Box Hill station, the number of railway officials and staff living in Dorking increased to 20[8].

When the LBSCR reached Dorking in 1867 a path was made to connect the two adjacent stations, starting from the bottom of the stairs to the Up side of the SER's Box Hill. Interchange traffic developed, which still continues today though most now walk round by road as the path is somewhat overgrown and unlit after dark. Nor, oddly, is it any quicker.

Deepdene station looking to Guildford, about 9 a.m. on 16 September 1963. There is little change from the 1900s picture except that the wooden platforms have been rebuilt with new supports and are now lit by gas. A can of water stands on the up platform ready to be taken to the Brockham crossing cottage by the next train. (Photo: Alan A. Jackson)

Exterior of Box Hill station SER (now Dorking (Deepdene)) looking north c. 1905. The board advertises trains for London Bridge, Cannon Street,Waterloo and Charing Cross. Carriage drive to The Deepdene at right foreground. The photographer is standing in London Road. (From a commercial postcard by G. Cheverton, Dorking)

Wartime manpower shortages led to closure of Box Hill SER from 1 January 1917 to 31 December 1918 inclusive, saving two staff, although it is apparent from photographs taken about ten years earlier that the complement was then somewhat larger.

Along with the buildings at Dorking Town, the decaying wooden structures at what was then called Deepdene were demolished at the end of 1969. After this the station became an unstaffed halt, equipped only with simple metal shelters. The old staircases survived until early in 1984, when they were replaced by unprotected steel stairs. Passengers now enter on the side of their chosen direction of travel.

This station remains quite busy, especially in the morning and early evening, and in term time it is used twice a day by large numbers of schoolchildren, some of whom, exploiting the absence of supervision, occupy their waiting time by attacking any surface with felt pens and paint sprays in an effort to express their deepest thoughts. Patronage at Deepdene has increased considerably since BR responded in 1986 to prolonged local agitation and added this call to all the hourly fast Reading-Gatwick Airport trains.

Westcott

Since at its nearest point, the RG&RR was almost a mile from its centre and linked only by the narrow Holehill Lane, no attempt was made to serve the prosperous and attractive village of Westcott, which stands astride the Guildford road about 2m west of Dorking. There was some residential growth here in the Victorian and Edwardian years, associated with the wealthier sections of the burgeoning middle class and those who served them. There is no doubt that if this had been GWR rather than SER territory, a halt would have been provided at the Holehill crossing place by 1914. However within a decade of that date, motor buses were running regularly along the main road and any pressure there might have been for such a stopping place quickly disappeared.

Something was indeed provided, but further west, and specifically tailored to a very specialised kind of traffic, born of the needs of war. In 1916 military rifle ranges were built on the north side of the railway at Coomb Farm and two wooden platforms were opened that November by the intermediate signal box. There was no regular service; trains called only to set down or pick up soldiers as required and Westcott Range Halt was not officially available for general public use. In any case it was some 15 minutes walk by awkward fieldpaths from Westcott Street.

Surrey Territorials continued to visit the range for a short period after World War 1 but in 1928, after parts of the halt had been damaged by fire, the SR Board decided to demolish the remains, noting that there had been no traffic 'in recent years'.

Services and Traffic on the Redhill-Reading Line

The line through Dorking and Box Hill (later Deepdene) has seen a great variety of traffic and services. For its first 115 or so years, variety and interest also prevailed for the railway observer in the steam locomotives and rolling stock employed, so much so that these deserve brief mention here, although those interested in such matters are referred to the bibliography for sources of greater detail.

Strange though it may seem today, there was at first a degree of competition for the Reading to London business between the SER and the GWR and also, later, with the LSWR for the traffic arising from the military complex around Aldershot. Despite the fact that the Reading to London distance by the GWR was a mere 36 miles compared with almost 69 by the SER via Dorking, through trains were worked over the latter route for many years. There were still 12 each way as late as 1918 and, such was the strength of railway tradition, one each way persisted until the early 1960s. This service resulted in London-bound trains facing in opposite directions at Guildford, a circumstance which, together with the multiplicity of destinations available at that station, may have explained a notice which could be seen there for many years:

DO NOT GET INTO ANY TRAIN WITHOUT FIRST ASKING THE OFFICIALS

The competition produced some very cheap fares from Reading to London via Dorking and also resulted in Dorking getting some faster workings than might otherwise have been the case. Thus in 1852 there was a train at 08.45 from Reading, calling only at Guildford, Shalford and Dorking, running non-stop from the latter to London Bridge, which was reached at 10.45. A return train at 18.00 followed a similar timing but stopped at Redhill instead of Dorking. In the following year there were three such trains in the Up direction and two Down. However a fares agreement with the GWR in 1858 brought an end to this competitive activity.

Then in the 1870s and again in 1895 there were brief outbreaks of competition with the LSWR for the military traffic between Aldershot and London. This temporarily gave Dorking some fast trains to the City. Otherwise the best trains were in the morning and evening business hours although these only ran fast between East Croydon and London Bridge.

At first the hopes of the RG&RR promoters for through traffic from the midlands, north and west were frustrated, partly due to the difference in track gauge at Reading which required transhipment of both goods and passengers. A standard gauge connection was eventually provided in 1858. Even then the GWR remained reluctant to exchange through trains, although a few passenger trains were run from the GWR through Dorking to the Kent coast between 1863 and 1866. Nothing more happened for another 30 years, but from 1897 Dorking became a stop on a new cross country service conveying through carriages from Merseyside and the Midlands to the Channel Ports of Dover and Folkestone. This led Dorking station staff to refer to these trains as the 'Contis' (Continentals). A more convenient connection to the GWR at Reading was put into use in December 1899 and after a brief gap in 1900-03, the Conti reappeared, running from Birkenhead to Deal and back. Withdrawn in 1916 and returning from 1922 a similar train ran each way daily between Birkenhead and Dover until 1939. It came back for the last time in October 1948 as a Birkenhead-Margate working, formed of SR stock throughout. By the 1960s it was running on summer Saturdays only, together with about six other through trains each way via Dorking. These long distance services disappeared altogether in September 1964. Apart from these through workings and the London services mentioned earlier, there was a basic stopping service, mostly between Reading and Tonbridge, but with some trains extended to Maidstone, Ramsgate, Dover and other places.

Between the wars the aspect of the line and its trains changed very little. The SECR electrification scheme of 1919 had included the section between Redhill and Dorking and as we shall see later there was an early SR proposal involving a new connection between the two lines at Dorking North. However nothing was done beyond the Southern's installation of electric working between Reigate and Redhill (and inwards to London) in July 1932.

We noticed earlier that the line through Dorking did not for many years command the best in passenger rolling stock. Until the early years of this century, after the SER had been taken into the South Eastern & Chatham Railways Joint Committee (SECR), the Redhill-Reading line was the haunt of some of the SER's most venerable carriages, enduring teak vehicles dating back to the 1850s. It was also known for its almost equally ancient locomotives, which included James I'Anson Cudworth's 2-4-0s built in 1859-75 without driver's cabs, and his 'Ironclads' of the same wheel arrangement built in 1876. Freight trains were largely hauled by Cudworth 0-6-0s until the more powerful Stirling 0-6-0s came on the scene around 1902. In World War 1, GWR 'Bulldog' and 'Duke' 4-4-0 locomotives worked to Redhill through Dorking, and some Great Northern Railway 2-4-0s were also to be seen, 15 of them borrowed to cope with the extra military traffic on the line.

Military traffic was important for many years. The Aldershot base, established in 1854-55, was soon served by the Reading-Guildford-Redhill line through sidings and a station at North Camp, on its east side. The expansion of this important army centre can be attributed in large part to the proximity of a usefully strategic railway giving excellent communication with the midlands and the north as well as the Channel Ports, avoiding London. And indeed the line through Dorking handled vast quantities of troops and military freight of all kinds in both world wars, these passing to and from many points as well as Aldershot. Ambulance trains were also seen, particularly in World War 1 and Dorking Town station was a favoured transhipment point for stretcher cases since it was on the level, facilitating their movement between trains and motor ambulances. In the second war, the line assumed even greater importance, owing to the vulnerability and actual bombing of the routes across London, and many trains were diverted through Dorking.

One outstanding achievement was the line's role in successful evacuation of British and allied troops from France via Dunkerque in 1940. Between 27 May and 4 June that year all normal traffic through Dorking was suspended, so that the railway could be given over entirely to the 24-hour working of troop trains westbound from Dover and Folkestone via Redhill. Empty stock was worked back eastbound as fast as it could be cleared. In that short period, no less than 565 heavily-loaded troop trains reached Redhill, 293 continuing westwards through Dorking. All were worked on an untimetabled basis and although the SR managed to muster a sufficiency of steam locos, carriages had to be borrowed from the other three companies.

One well-remembered train of World War 2 was the London & North Eastern Railway buffet car service between Newcastle and Ashford (Kent), introduced in 1940. In the northbound direction, this left Ashford at 08.45, calling at Dorking and arriving at Reading at 11.50, finally reaching Newcastle-on-Tyne at 20.45. Intended for service men and women proceeding to and from leave, its length often reached 13 or more corridor coaches. Loading to upwards of 435 tons, it posed a formidable challenge for its usual motive power, a Southern U1 2-6-0, since the long climb towards Gomshall had to be attempted after stopping at Deepdene. This train, whose predominantly military passengers would good-humouredly make room for the civilian traveller, ran until the end of 1944, when it was diverted to Southampton Docks.

The Guildford-Redhill route also saw heavy freight traffic in World War 2, much of it transfers between the GWR and the SR at Redhill and Tonbridge. To facilitate its working, a new marshalling yard was built at Shalford and a new signalbox and sidings at Buckland. Gomshall signalbox was also renewed. The emergency wartime spur between the two railways at Dorking will be mentioned later. As the war came to an end, there were many demobilisation trains through Dorking, bringing men back from the Far and Middle East via the 'Medloc' rail route through France and the short Channel crossing from Calais to Dover.

With the resumption of peace, both passenger and freight traffic and services through Dorking at first settled down much to the pre-war pattern. GWR locomotives, 2-6-0s and 4-6-0s, which had returned to the

23

line in 1938, were to continue to be regular visitors until the 1960s. The SECR Stirling F1 4-4-0s and D class 4-4-0s commonly used on passenger trains through to the 1930s were gradually replaced by Maunsell Moguls. The latter, first arriving on the line in 1924, were based at Redhill, Guildford and Reading sheds over four decades. SR 'Schools' 4-4-0s and BR standard class 4 2-6-0s were also regulars. In June 1963 BR diesel locomotives took over most of the freight workings, passenger steam continuing for another 18 months, making the line through Dorking one of the last outposts of regular steam working on the former SR system. Long-familiar sounds echoing across the hills as hard-worked steam locos pounded and struggled up from the Mole basin through Dorking were to disappear virtually overnight late in 1965 when the last of the few remaining steam freight workings was withdrawn. In accordance with tradition, the line was home to ancient SECR 'birdcage' compartment stock until finally replaced with more modern former SR and new BR corridor stock in the 1950s.

Twilight of steam on the Reading-Redhill line. SR Mogul no. 31790 on an Up train at Brockham Crossing, looking to Dorking on 2 January 1965. (Photo: Alan A. Jackson)

By the early 1960s passenger traffic on stopping trains between Redhill and Guildford had fallen below the 5000 journeys a week which Beeching had set as the criterion for retention of passenger service on secondary and branch lines. Both Dorking Town (now West) and Deepdene stations therefore appeared in the slaughter list appended to the notorious Beeching Report of 1963[9]. Happily the large amount of mail handled at Reading, Guildford, Redhill and Tonbridge played some part in ensuring the continuation of the intermediate passenger services. From 4 January 1965 a new regular hourly service of diesel-electric multiple-unit trains superseded the steam trains in the hope that this might revitalise the line.

The trains consisted of two cars of the narrow width Hastings line stock of 1957 together with a control trailer of normal width. This discrepancy in dimensions brought them the nickname 'Tadpoles'. There were not only faster journeys, but for the first time ever, a tidy unified service between Reading and Tonbridge, giving a basic hourly interval with some extra trains at peak hours, the latter of ordinary corridor stock hauled by Class 33 diesel locomotives. A notice exhibited at the time suggested that the decision to retain and modernise this through cross-country link would only be justified if more passengers used it, many new ones being required if its future were to be assured. Whilst there was some increase in patronage, the new business was for some years at a disappointing level. The spread of car ownership in the 1960s was such that it bit deeply into the use of all types of public transport for other than commuter journeys, especially so in this prosperous area.

Sensibly, further economies were made. From 5 November 1967, tickets were checked and issued by conductor-guards on the trains and staff were removed from all stations between Reigate and Guildford exclusive. The new trains had not at first called at Dorking Town on Sundays but this was changed, since it made little sense once the station had become unstaffed. Regular use of loco haulage on passenger trains ceased in May 1977, releasing crews and saving rolling stock costs. A programme of signalling modernisation, which included track circuiting, colour light signals and automatic barriers at road level crossings, was completed in 1983. All signal boxes between Shalford and Reigate were closed. Finally, for a time, Sunday morning trains were withdrawn in the winter months, a decision fortunately soon reversed.

Then, although it still required a subsidy, the fortunes of the line's passenger business changed. This improvement began on 12 May 1980 with the introduction of a fast hourly service of BR standard 3-car diesel units between Reading and Gatwick Airport, supplementing the stopping trains between Reading and Redhill. Instantly popular with air travellers and others, this service at first ignored Dorking, but after what was beginning to look like fruitless pressure from Dorking interests, BR finally agreed it should call at Deepdene from May 1986. However this important improvement was not attained without some severe reductions in the all-stations service between Guildford and Tonbridge which deprived Dorking Town (now West) of its regular hourly train each way on week-days and of any Sunday service.

An interesting recent development and a reminder of the line's strategic value, was the introduction from 16 May 1988 of a new Travelling Post Office train from Dover to Manchester via Dorking. With the familiar red Royal Mail cars and hauled by a diesel locomotive, this leaves Redhill (where late letters can be posted on the train) at 21.16 each weekday. There is a corresponding return working.

25

Freight traffic, once so important, began to decline in the 1970s, dwindling to a few roadstone trains to Merstham and Gatwick, an occasional oil tanker or bulk cement train and one or two inter-regional parcels workings. The 1980s saw further erosion and there is now very little freight apart from the railway's own engineering trains.

A word should be said about the line's future, which could change its use dramatically. The Channel Tunnel is now being built for opening in May 1993 and the development of new traffics and services through it may well bring about electrification and improvement of the railway between Redhill and Reading, perhaps including a much-needed flyover at Redhill to avoid reversal of all trains moving between Tonbridge and Reading.

The intention of the 1846 RG&RR promoters that their line should link Europe with the rest of Britain avoiding London thus becomes surprisingly relevant almost 150 years on. But the future of the Redhill-Reading railway as a Channel Tunnel link for non-London traffic will depend upon whether the capital can be found to upgrade and modernise it to meet these new demands in a manner fully competitive with road transport, using the best in modern railway technology. Public attitudes in the affected areas, expressed in a manner and strength to which politicians feel they must respond will also be important. In this respect it is to be hoped that public opinion will recognise that railway modernisation would certainly be far less damaging to the sensitive and already-embattled Surrey environment than the alternative of providing new and wider motorways.

The Mickleham Valley Invaded

Dorking's second railway, running south through the Mickleham Valley to cross the Deepdene hills at the west end of Betchworth Park, is perhaps the best known, since it has always been the busiest, offering as it does the most direct route to London. For that reason it now possesses the town's only staffed station.

North of Dorking, the alignment followed was that chosen for schemes of the 1830s for a London to Brighton line and, as already mentioned, for the abortive 1846 proposal for a railway from Epsom to Leatherhead, Dorking, Shalford, Havant and Portsmouth. There was also an unsuccessful project in 1838-9 for a London & Dorking Railway, branching off the London & Southampton at Wimbledon and following much the same route as the present line via Worcester Park and Epsom. As built, the line through the Mickleham Valley did in fact become part of the LBSCR's rather tortuous route from London to Portsmouth via Horsham and Arundel, continuing to carry main line trains, latterly electrified, until the end of the 1970s. Today its status south of Dorking is alas much diminished, its use limited, thanks to the emergence of Gatwick as a lucrative traffic centre.

The LBSCR and the LSWR had opened a joint line from Epsom to Leatherhead in 1859, sharing a station in the latter town. It was not long before an independent Horsham, Dorking & Leatherhead Railway (HDLR) was promoted by local interests. These came mainly from Horsham, but their spokesman was John Labouchere, owner of Broome Hall and father of Henry, the famous journalist and politician. The LBSCR was soon involved, agreeing to provide stations and track materials. That company, which had been quick to see the value of the route as an alternative approach to Portsmouth and to Brighton (via Steyning), was ready to oppose with a scheme of its own if the HDLR was not prepared to spend money on a main line standard double track line.

The HDLR was sanctioned in July 1862, but only between the SER at Dorking and Horsham, since the local company was now in financial difficulties. At Dorking the connection to the SER was to be just east of Box Hill (now Dorking (Deepdene)) station. Powers were given to the LBSCR to contribute to the cost, to work and maintain the line, appoint three directors and take £75,000 in shares of the £120,000 capital.

Unable to solve its financial problems, the HDLR now turned to the LBSCR, which was enabled by the LBSCR (Additional Powers) Act of 1864 to absorb the local company on completion of the works. Determined to seize the route as its own, and concerned that the SER might encourage use of the connection at Dorking, the LBSCR had secured parliamentary authority to build the four-mile section from Leatherhead to Dorking in July 1863 and this was completed and opened on 11 March 1867. Delays in construction of the 13½ miles onwards to Horsham, largely related to problems with the clay subsoil of the Weald and the wet and sandy Betchworth Tunnel, postponed the opening of that section until 1 May, from which date it formed part of the LBSCR under the provisions of the 1864 Act. At first the basic through service consisted of about four trains each way daily between London Bridge and Brighton via the Steyning line but from 1878 the through service at Dorking became London Bridge to Bognor and Portsmouth, working over the 1868 line from Sutton to Peckham Rye. Victoria portions were joined/split at Mitcham Junction, then, from 1888, at Sutton.

In accordance with its Act, the HDLR had constructed the 21-chain (422.52 metre) single track connection to the SER on the east side of Dorking, near the point where the new line passed beneath the Redhill-Guildford tracks. The junction with the SER was about 150yd east of Box Hill (now Dorking (Deepdene)) station and the connection with the HDLR/LBSCR, which the latter named Dorking Junction, was almost half a mile south of the new LBSCR station at Dorking, at a point just north of the bridge under the Dorking to Reigate road. It was not in the LBSCR's interests, as the new owners, to encourage the use of this link, though it was no doubt also realised that parliament placed some importance on it, in view of its potential strategic value for moving troops quickly from Aldershot to meet any threat of an invader landing on the Sussex coast and moving up across the Weald. Such considerations may explain why it remained intact but virtually unused for so many years. On at least one occasion it did carry Derby Week race specials from the Tonbridge-Hastings line to Epsom, involving two time-consuming reversals at Dorking but there were never any regular workings over it.

Around 1900 the junction with the SER was severed, the remainder, together with a parallel siding which terminated 30 yards south of the SER embankment, becoming a berthing point for empty carriage stock. After the provision of extra carriage sidings in the LSBCR station at Dorking, the two tracks were used to hold trucks of hay cut from the railway banks and cuttings before storing it in ricks nearby until sold. The 1914 25-inch Ordnance Survey map shows a crane here which may have been used for this traffic.

In 1926 both the siding and the remains of the connecting spur were removed but the connection was restored on 3 September 1941 to allow for diversion of traffic following bomb damage to either route through Dorking. In practice this need never arose and the track was dismantled for the final time early in 1946. Subsequently some of the land was sold and in 1976 it was partly built over to form what is now Chester Close. The rest is now very difficult to trace on the ground.

Soon after its formation in 1923, the SR proposed another connection between the two lines, on the north side, facing Redhill. Parliamentary powers for this were obtained in 1924 and some of the necessary land was bought. It was planned to use this link for a new electric service from London to Dorking via Epsom, returning via Redhill and East Croydon and vice versa, but the idea was dropped before any work was started.

The route taken by the LBSCR's Leatherhead to Horsham line through the picturesque Mickleham Valley proved expensive to build since the railway company found itself facing Thomas Grissell, an experienced railway contractor, as owner of most of the required land. Grissell, who had retired to Norbury Park in 1850, knew only too well how to ensure the railway passed through his estate with the least possible environmental damage, securing an agreement which exacted both this and the maximum possible compensation[10]. He required ornamental structures throughout, so the three viaducts over the river Mole were given coloured brickwork, cornices and decorative cast-iron parapets and the 524-yard Mickleham Tunnel had to be bored through the chalk without any vertical shafts, its portals given architectural treatment. Similar care had to be lavished on the appearance of the intermediate

28

station at West Humble, to be referred to later. To screen the railway from view, mature ornamental trees were to be planted and the alignment also had to take this requirement into account. The success of Grissell's stipulations can be seen today, particularly at the point where the Mole curves round the south escarpment, with the railway plunging dramatically from the tunnel on to a viaduct. Juxtaposition of tunnel, viaduct and steep-sided river here provide spectacular scenery, reminiscent of Switzerland. South of Westhumble, the owner of the Denbies Estate insisted on similar ornamentation, taking his cue from Grissell, but Henry Thomas Hope, owner of the Deepdene Estate, through which the line would pass between the SER and a point just south of the Betchworth Tunnel, required only flat iron fencing, sporting rights over the line and no shafts from the surface to the tunnel, for which only an easement was granted.

Mickleham Crossing and Tunnel, looking to Leatherhead, 21 July 1981. (Photo: Alan A. Jackson)

Just south of Mickleham Tunnel, the line crossed Swanworth Lane on the level and a pair of prettily-gabled cottages were provided on the Down side for gatekeepers and other railway staff. In 1891 an inter-mediate signal box was erected here on the Up side, south of the crossing, and was apparently at one time painted green all over at the request of the then owner of Norbury Park, Leopold Salomons, in order to minimise its impact on his view from the house and park above[12]. In 1971 this little box was closed and demolished after the road had been downgraded to a foot crossing. Just south of here is another of the ornamental viaducts over the Mole, skew-arched, and built like the others to allow the river to

29

expand at times of flood to a width of 120ft. An interesting feature to be observed here from the train is the abandoned ox-bow in the field, marking the course of the river before it was diverted to allow a clear flow under the railway.

Approaching Dorking, the alignment was brought as near as possible to the town, given that further progress southwards faced the barrier of greensand hills of the Deepdene and Betchworth Parks. Since a more direct southward route would have entailed a long and costly tunnel, this in any case ruling out a station sited at the east end of the High Street, there was no alternative other than a wide sweep west or east.

LBSCR Portsmouth to London Bridge train approaching Dorking c. 1910. The photograph is taken from the SER embankment looking towards Betchworth Tunnel and shows the sharp curve towards the bridge under the Reigate Road. Dorking advance starter signal in left foreground. (Photographer unknown)

The latter was chosen. There was also the problem of joining up with the line from Horsham, which had been laid out to make a reasonable junction with the SER rather than to run on to Leatherhead. These restraints produced a reverse curve on a rising gradient, an awkward arrangement for Down steam trains, especially those struggling to get away after stopping at Dorking station. Pixham Lane, which joined the Reigate Road opposite Punchbowl Lane, was diverted eastwards at its southern end to avoid an expensive skew road bridge over the through line and the connection to the SER. The extreme eastern end of the Deepdene ridge was then penetrated by a dead straight tunnel of 385 yards, through which the gradient reached its maximum rise of 1 in 80. Named after the Park whose western end it traversed, Betchworth Tunnel was to prove troublesome. There had been some falls of sand during its construction, delaying completion of the line, as already mentioned. Worse was to come. On 27 July 1887, the Wednesday of Goodwood Week, shortly after a train had passed through, the roof and walls suddenly gave way, running sand bursting through the lining like water until both tracks were completely blocked. Fortunately the obstruction was seen and the next trains due were stopped in time but the heavy return traffic from the Races had to be diverted via Three Bridges. The line between Horsham and Dorking was to remain closed from that morning until 1 March 1888 whilst the tunnel was virtually rebuilt.

LBSCR London Bridge Portsmouth train, hauled by no. 204 *Telford*, about to pass under the Reigate Road road bridge at Pixham, Dorking, c. 1905. The remains of the connection to the SER line can be seen above the first three coaches. (Photo: Courtesy Bluebell Railway Archive)

The four and a half miles between Dorking Junction and Holmwood station contained some features worthy of note. Just beyond the tunnel and 150yd north of the bridge over Tilehurst Lane, a ground frame and hut were provided in 1908 to control one distant and one stop signal either side. Manned only at Bank Holidays and other times of heavy traffic, this was not replaced after it had been burnt down in 1928. Nearby, on the Up side, is a track paralleling hut erected for the electrification of 1938. Further south, at Lodge Lane, a bridle way crossed the line on the level. Before 1877 the gates here were worked by hand, the signals controlled from a small ground frame. The LBSCR built two cement-rendered staff cottages east of the line on the Holmwood side of the ground frame. A brick signalbox of standard latter-day LBSCR pattern, named Lodge Farm Intermediate, was erected here in 1877 and manned from 07.00 to 22.00 on weekdays. Its Saxby & Farmer frame had six levers (two of them spare), controlling one distant and one stop signal in each direction. There were catch points on the Dorking side to derail any broken away portion of a loose-coupled Down freight

31

running back downhill. The five and a quarter mile ascent from Dorking continued to beyond Holmwood, with a long stretch of 1 in 100 beginning at Lodge Farm.

Lodge Farm Crossing from Horsham-Victoria train, looking north, 21 July 1981. (Photo: Alan A. Jackson)

Queen Victoria's funeral train, running late on its way from Gosport to London (Victoria) on Saturday 2 February 1901, came down this bank towards Dorking at around 75 m.p.h., the vibration being enough to cause the attendants to fear that the royal coffin might topple from its plinth to the floor of the saloon. Their concern was not lessened when, on entering the tunnel, the driver made a sharp brake application for the Dorking curves. No doubt the impression of instability was heightened because the track just north of Lodge Farm tended to be somewhat spongy where it crossed a depression which collects water from the surrounding hills. The funeral train, consisting of the five LBSCR royal saloons, Queen Victoria's GWR saloon containing the coffin, and a bogie First and bogie First and Second Class composite, was hauled by 'B4' 4-4-0 no. 54 *Empress*.

Later Lodge Farm was downgraded to a crossing box and its instruments were removed in 1938 when colour light signals, controlled from Dorking, were extended as far as here. The gatekeeper then used a plunger and lever to control the gates after obtaining permission from Dorking. Finally, from the end of January 1986, the crossing was closed to road traffic and the box was demolished. Blackbrook substation, erected for the 1938 electrification between Dorking and Horsham, stands just north of Lodge Farm, on the Up side. Towards Horsham, the line curves gently southwestwards to serve Holmwood and Ockley, passing under the bridge built in 1969 for the then new A24 Holmwood By Pass.

32

Another Station for The Town

On its new line of 1867 the LBSCR erected a substantial station at the point where the tracks came nearest to Dorking, 25½ miles from London Bridge, 23¾ from Victoria and 4m 1 chain from Leatherhead. Approached by a 165-yard drive from the main Dorking to London road (now the A24), it was about 300 yards north of the SER's Box Hill station.

Dorking station, LBSCR, 1867. What is now the Lincoln Road underline bridge is at the extreme right and to the left of this is the first signal box, raised on stilts. The artist has wonderfully exaggerated the height of Box Hill. (Engraving for *Illustrated London News*, 1867)

Dorking, LBSCR, Station Approach and *Star & Garter Hotel*, c. 1905. Note the 'formal' gate at left to mark the private status of the approach road. (From a Kingsway Real Photo Series postcard)

Less ornamental in character than its sister stations at Leatherhead and West Humble, the structure was nevertheless pleasing and not intrusive against the gentle green eminence of Box Hill in the background. On the Up side, it consisted of two storeys, the upper one for the stationmaster's domestic accommodation. The architect was Charles H. Driver, also responsible for the other two stations and, with Charles H. Rew, for Dorking's ugly public hall of 1872. Builder of all these was a local man, William Shearburn, who may have contributed some personal touches to the stations. A contemporary account of the new line[13] mentions his name and comments that the station work was not expensive 'as the effect is given by the judicious mixture of materials and grouping of details, so as to give picturesque outlines and a pleasing elevation'. In similar style on the Down side was a single storey block containing waiting rooms and lavatories for both sexes, this reached by a narrow subway between the centres of the platforms.

In its basic arrangement and facilities, Dorking did not differ greatly from other LBSCR small country town stations of the period and the detailed layout would have been the responsibility of the office of the company's chief engineer, W. Jacomb Hood. A three-road goods yard was provided. This had a brick−built goods shed, five ton crane and four sidings on the Up or west side, a road vehicle loading dock, stabling for delivery cart horses, a tank house feeding locomotive water cranes on the two platforms and a small locomotive yard with siding to ash disposal pit and coaling stage, turntable and a wooden shed with two roads. This little engine shed was badly damaged in a 1921 gale, but the inspection pits remained for another three years after which the space was used for additional sidings. The whole of this area, approximately that now occupied by the present main car park, covered about two and a half acres.

In the station itself there were crossovers between the running lines at each end and a trailing connection from the country end of the Down platform to a carriage siding running parallel with the back of the platform to a buffer stop just south of the abutment of the road bridge. Points placed a short distance from each end of this siding served a long engine release loop.

At the country end on the Up side, between the platform and the bridge over the bridleway to Pixham there was a wooden signal box on stilts. In 1877 as part of the signalling modernisation between Dorking and Horsham, a new box on a brick base called Dorking North was erected at the London end, again on the Up side, between the road bridge and the trailing connection from the Up running line to the goods and loco yards. This contained a 31-lever frame and was built high enough for the signalmen to look over the road bridge towards West Humble. Until 1926 the 1867 box, renamed Dorking South, remained in use for shunting movements.

Dorking LBSCR looking to London c. 1910. Lines to goods yard and locomotive depot at left. D1 0-4-2T *Belmont* stands at the Up Through platform with a stopping train for Victoria. The opposite face is the Up Bay platform. (Photographer unknown)

No less than 19 railway staff could be mustered to assemble at Dorking LBSCR for a photo-call at a quiet moment between trains c. 1910. The Stationmaster is third from the left. The camera is looking to London. Among the many posters are two giving details of rail and sea facilities to Bavaria, Austria and Holland. (Redhill Photo Co.)

Since the station was a good half mile from the centre of the town, cab proprietors have always enjoyed a fair trade. A horse bus service was tried, but in 1893, when asked to restore it, the LBSCR refused, stating that the original service had resulted in a loss of £100 a year for the proprietor.

Around 1901, with commuter and holiday traffic expanding, three more carriage sidings were laid down on the east side of the station parallel with the original. A new crossover was placed on the London side of the road bridge about the same time. From an earlier date a bay road had been set into the Up platform at the London end for terminating trains.

An effort was made by the LBSCR in 1907 to stimulate local traffic south of Dorking and east of Horsham. Railmotor units were introduced, consisting of a Stroudley 'D' class 0-4-2T between two coaches or an A1 0-6-0T with a single 'Balloon' coach. These could be driven from either end and ran in and out of a bay at the north end of Horsham station, those to and from Dorking making convenient connections with the service between Horsham and Three Bridges.

Mention of the 'D' class tanks recalls a pleasant practice of the LBSCR. Certain locomotives were given names of places served by the company then stationed at sheds in or near the area. Thus no. 229 *Dorking* was often seen here, together with her sisters 290 *Denbies* and 291 *Deepdene*, all kept in resplendent condition by their allocated crews. From 1873 when they were first introduced, until well into the SR era, Dorking shed always had a complement of four or five engines of this class, mostly finding work on the London stopping trains. Other LBSCR engines with local names were 'D' class *Ranmore* and *Mickleham*, allocated to Epsom shed, and 'A' class 'Terrier' 0-6-0T *Boxhill*, which became the Brighton Works pilot in 1920 and is now in the National Railway Museum[14].

LBSCR 0-4-2T no. 229 *Dorking* at her home base c. 1905. Box Hill and Pixham Lane in background. (Courtesy Bluebell Railway Archive)

The 'D' class tank locomotives at Dorking were worked hard, especially after the introduction of the eight hour day on the railways in 1919. Around 1920 these engines were manned by three crews in the course of a day. On a typical weekday diagram, the loco would leave Dorking at 07.00 with a London Bridge train, returning from there about two hours later with a Horsham train, running via Epsom and Dorking, the enginemen being relieved at Dorking by the middle turn driver and fireman. After a short pause at Horsham, the locomotive then worked to Brighton via Steyning, leaving again early in the afternoon for Horsham, Dorking and Victoria with a short wait at Dorking when the late turn crew took over. From Victoria the engine took the Victoria portion of the 19.20 Portsmouth train as far as Sutton, calling only at Clapham Junction. Then, after a wait, it ran light to Epsom, returning to Victoria in time to haul the 22.58 to Dorking, which was reached at midnight. After shunting the empty train away, the engine was returned to the shed where the fire was cleaned and left ready for the early turn men who would arrive at 06.15. This diagram involved some 210 miles of running every weekday except on Mondays. On that day the boiler was washed out with cold water and refilled. Sundays saw the same engine on a more relaxed routine: first running light to Horsham, working a Horsham-London train via Dorking and returning to Dorking about midday. After standing by in the afternoon, it would run light to Holmwood to take a train from there to London, returning with another and reaching Dorking around 23.00[15].

Electrification and Rebuilding

With the formation of the Southern Railway at the beginning of 1923 it became necessary to distinguish the Dorking LBSCR station from the others and from 9 July it was renamed Dorking North. Although the 'North' was officially dropped by BR from 6 May 1968, the old name, still to be seen on road signs, continues to be used in the town.

Dorking was an early beneficiary of the Southern Railway's extensive electrification programme. From Sunday 12 July 1925 electric trains working on the SR standard 600 Volt third rail system operated a regular interval service twice an hour, seven days a week, between Dorking and Waterloo, covering the 22¼ miles in 44 minutes. This timing was soon increased by making calls at all stations. These Waterloo trains were in addition to the steam services to Victoria and London Bridge, which continued much as before.

At a cost of £6,300 a terminal bay was constructed early in 1925 at the back of the Down platform, which was opened up, widened and given a canopy to form a new platform face, numbered 3. About the same time two extra carriage sidings were added to the east side, making a total of six. An electric traction substation containing two 1,250 kW rotary converters was built on the Down side, near the A24 bridge.

About 1926 the old Up side bay was lifted and in 1950 the space was filled in with ballast to platform level to provide standing for an LBSCR saloon coach body which was to serve as a cycle store.

A further electric service started on 3 March 1929, running hourly to and from London Bridge via Mitcham Junction and Tulse Hill, twice an hour at peak periods. The 25½ miles were covered in 53 minutes and the irregular steam trains to and from Victoria continued. For this extra service, the carriage sidings on the Down side were all electrified and the conductor rails on the running lines extended about 300 yards towards Horsham to allow for shunting in and out of these sidings. On the same day, a reorganised steam push and pull service began to work between Dorking and Horsham, with some journeys extended to Guildford via Cranleigh. For this, a short bay was cut into the country end of platform 3 at Dorking North.

Further improvements came in 1938 when the Mid-Sussex lines were electrified. From 3 July, when the full public service started, the town was served by 11 fast buffet car trains each way daily between London (Victoria) and Bognor and Portsmouth. To and from London, outside the peak periods, these stopped only at Sutton, giving Dorking passengers a 37 minute timing over the 23¾ congested miles. At peak hours, the privileged Dorking commuters gained a non stop buffet car run to and from Victoria, taking only 34 minutes.

With the 1938 electrification, the twice hourly Waterloo-Dorking North stopping service was extended southwards, one an hour to Holmwood, the other to Horsham, whilst the hourly London Bridge-Dorking North stopping trains were also extended to Horsham. The steam push and pull services were now withdrawn but until January 1964 steam locomotives were still occasionally seen at Dorking North on parcels, freight and special trains.

Apart from wartime, this excellent electric service continued little changed for 40 years, the fast trains becoming hourly from June 1962. Sadly for Dorking, the development of Gatwick Airport produced a major new source of railway revenue, causing BR to divert all the fast Mid-Sussex line trains via Three Bridges and the Airport station. All-day weekday fast trains disappeared from Dorking North from May 1978 with the remaining peak hour and Saturday workings following in May 1984. In compensation, some services between London and Dorking were slightly speeded up by omitting some station stops.

From the 1950s the spread of car ownership and television reduced patronage outside the rush hour. This brought about a deterioration in the formerly generous electric stopping services. As early as 1958 the

38

Holmwood service was cut back to run to and from Epsom only, leaving Dorking with three instead of four trains an hour through the day. In July 1967 the basic service to stations between Dorking and Horsham was reduced to hourly, Dorking's three trains an hour becoming two to and from Victoria (one fast) and one to and from Waterloo. From 5 May 1969, intermediate stations between Dorking and Horsham lost their trains except at the peak hours, Dorking still retaining its three trains an hour each way. With the disappearance of the regular main line services in May 1978, Dorking was down to two trains an hour each way through the day, and since mid 1987 one of these, to and from Victoria, has run semi-fast, covering the 25¾ miles in 39 or 40 minutes.

Today cross-platform interchange and connections at Epsom normally allow a choice of either London terminus every half hour on weekdays and Saturdays. On Sundays there is but one train an hour between London and Dorking. From May 1986 there were virtually no trains south of Dorking outside the peak periods Mondays to Friday, apart from a few midday and Saturday trains serving Holmwood and Horsham only but some improvement was made from October 1987, with trains roughly every two hours (calling at Holmwood only) outside the peak periods.

The 1938 signal box and 1867 station buildings on 5 August 1979, looking south. (Photo: Alan A. Jackson)

The mid-Sussex electrification of 1938 saw some structural alterations to Dorking station, costing a total of £30,225 at 1938 prices. Most prominent was the new red brick and concrete signalbox in the streamlined marine style

39

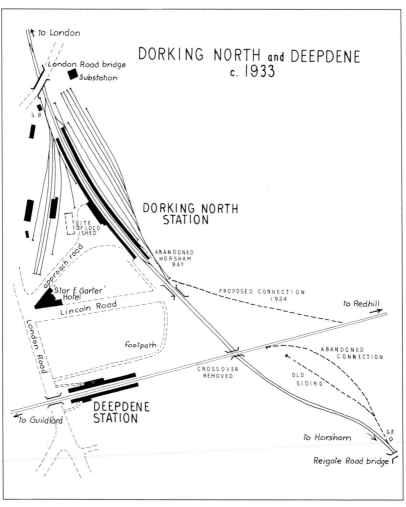

To London

London Road bridge

Substation

DORKING NORTH and DEEPDENE
c. 1933

S B

DORKING NORTH
STATION

SITE
OF LOCO
SHED

ABANDONED
HORSHAM
BAY

approach road

Star & Garter
Hotel

Lincoln Road

PROPOSED CONNECTION
1924

To Redhill

London Road

Footpath

CROSSOVER
REMOVED

ABANDONED
CONNECTION

OLD
SIDING

DEEPDENE
STATION

To Guildford

To Horsham

G.F.

Reigate Road bridge

of the period, bearing the town's name in large letters, which came into use on 15 May 1938. *The Railway Gazette* described this and the sister boxes at Horsham, Arundel and Bognor as of 'an imposing design, fit symbols of the coming of electric traction to the quiet . . . countryside'. The Dorking cabin controlled colour light signals on the newly track-circuited stretch from Mickleham Crossing to Lodge Farm Crossing, this being extended to Leatherhead in October 1971. There were position-light junction-indicators for diverging routes and points remote from the box were power-operated. Most points however remained rod-worked from the new mechanical frame and shunt signals were moved by wires.

In the station, platforms were lengthened to 800ft to take the 12-car main line trains, work which required the widening of the underbridge

Dorking, looking to Leatherhead, 10.35 a.m. 5 August 1974. Several slates are missing from the roof of the doomed 1867 building on the Up platform. Three trains wait in the sidings for the evening peak period. (Photo: Alan A. Jackson)

carrying the line over Lincoln Road and the abolition of the Horsham bay at the country end of the Down platform, from which the track had been removed some time earlier. Finally the Down terminal line in platform 3 was connected to the Down main line at the Horsham end to form an electrified loop. Trains could then terminate in the Down main or Down loop and the Down line could also be used as an Up loop if required.

The 1925 substation was re-equipped with an unattended mercury arc rectifier, provision being made for its extension in the event of the electrification of the Redhill-Guildford line.

Dorking did not escape the general decline in freight traffic in the 1950s. Despite the closure of the yard at Dorking Town, Dorking North became unviable and was closed on 7 November 1966. For a time some tracks remained in use as an engineer's depot before the space was converted to a rail passengers' car park. Before this, the all-conquering car had demanded hard-surfacing of the stationmaster's garden, which used to run from the main station entrance down to Lincoln Road, parallel to the railway. Half was lost, then all of it, and finally the first section of the footpath to Deepdene station was taken in.

The remaining buildings of 1867, the water tank house and stables, survived in the main car park area until January 1986. Despite the loss of freight, parcels traffic at the station continued and today there is a thriving business in Red Star parcels, for which facilities were provided when the Up side was rebuilt in 1982.

Exterior of the 1867 LBSCR station at Dorking on 5 August 1979. (Photo: Alan A. Jackson)

In January 1975 *The Dorking Advertiser* reported that the attractive 1867 station building was 'falling down'. It was said that maintenance had been neglected, no-one was using the living accommodation, there was dry rot and the bricks were crumbling. Nevertheless, the old buildings survived until 1980, when a deal was concluded for a new structure exploiting the commercial value of the site. Designed by Gordon Lavington A.R.I.B.A. in association with the BR Southern Region Architect's Department, this contained offices for the local firm of Biwater on two upper storeys and a three-storey north wing. On the ground floor, parallel with the Up platform, were a newsagents' and confectioners' shop, taxi office, ticket hall and office, railway staff rooms and lavatories. This building's somewhat drab and flat-roofed, red-brick bulk fitted fairly quietly against the background of Box Hill but it lacked the modest elegance of its predecessor. All work was finished by the end of 1982, the new ticket office opening on 23 August that year. Towards the end of 1986, the remaining LBSCR buildings, on the Down side, were taken down, to be replaced by a flat-roofed steel and glass structure containing a waiting and staff room. This sheltered the stairs to a refurbished subway which now forms the only relic of the original station on the site.

More recently the station has been included in the long-line public address system which is part of the major Waterloo area resignalling programme, due for completion in autumn 1989. When this is finished, public announcements will be made from the new signalling centre at

Wimbledon, where a panel will control all movements as far out as Dorking. Dorking's 1938 signal box will however remain as a fringe box, controlling the line south to Horsham.

Boxhill & Westhumble

At a point less than a mile from Dorking, Thomas Grissell insisted on having his own station. As it was *his* station, it naturally had to be the most ornate of any on the line, so Charles Driver designed a building with steeply-pitched roofs of patterned tiles, exposed gable timbers and, at the entrance, a huge porch with hammerbeam roof supported on heavy decorated columns. A pyramidal turret topped by decorative grille and weather vane added a suggestion of French chateau style. Passengers reached the Up side by a covered footbridge, where they waited in a small single storey building matching the main one. This little pavilion (which also contained lavatories) is now boarded up against vandalism, the roof of the footbridge has long since gone and the canopies have been altered, but otherwise the station remains much as built, protected by Grade II listing at the Department of the Environment.

A goods yard was unnecessary owing to the proximity to Dorking. The small signal box originally erected at the London end of the Up platform against the road bridge over the line had disappeared by the 1920s.

Box Hill, LBSCR soon after its opening in 1867, looking towards Dorking. (Original in Surrey Local History Library, Guildford; negative courtesy Ronald Shepperd)

43

The position of the station was largely governed by one of Grissell's many stipulations, which required the railway immediately south of the tunnel to be carried as far eastwards as possible to screen the view from Norbury Park, then as far westwards as possible to avoid interference with the West Humble infants' school and other buildings. One or two cottages on the south side of the road had to be demolished and some cutting into the rising ground on the west side was necessary.

At first this station was named West Humble for Box Hill. It was in the very centre of the small village but three quarters of a mile from the bottom of Box Hill. In November 1870 the LBSCR started to call it Box Hill & Burford Bridge, then in May 1896 simply Box Hill but in December 1904 it became Box Hill & Burford Bridge again. Finally in September 1958 BR decided upon Boxhill and Westhumble, running both words together to conform with current usage.

In former times the stationmaster here enjoyed several perks in addition to the privilege of living in such a fine building and taking tips from the gentry passing to and from Norbury Park and Polesden Lacey. Until May 1931 he was also the Westhumble postmaster, transacting this business from the railway ticket office and using his minions to deliver public telegrams received on the railway's telegraph instrument. It must have been difficult for him to keep his temper, coping with demands for two shilling postal orders or a couple of penny stamps as the vast crowds of Cockney Bank Holidaymakers thronged the platforms, but perhaps the people of Westhumble had the sense to keep well away from the station area at such times. Another of the SM's diversions, aided by his wife, was to serve teas to ramblers and holidaymakers, if fine in the station house garden, otherwise in his sitting room overlooking the Down platform. Not content with all this activity, the SM also sold newspapers to passengers and others on behalf of the manager of the W. H. Smith bookstall at Dorking North station. Until the 1920s the station staff handled milk from Chapel Farm and Home Farm to be despatched to London every morning by passenger train in 17-gallon churns. Once as many as four men were employed but now one man or woman suffices, working on Monday to Friday mornings only.

Grissell also obtained a right to stop any train on request, a privilege that was still being exercised in 1910 by Leopold Salomons, who had bought Norbury Park in 1890. Westhumblians who spotted him or any of his family at Victoria would risk boarding a fast train, knowing it would probably stop. This concession, along with many other similar ones, was abolished by the BR Act of 1963 but it is a curious fact that until quite recent years, the station was served by an excellent semi-fast late rush hour train, with a similar return working in the evening from Victoria, which suggests that someone influential in railway circles may have used the station.

Until recent economies took their toll of staff, Boxhill passengers were pampered. The railmen lent out umbrellas and comforting reading matter and would telephone wives when trains were running late.

For many years, like Dorking, this station saw a considerable pleasure traffic from April to September, especially at the Easter, Whit and August Bank Holiday weekends, when the platforms would be so choked with the cheap and cheerful element of South London that extra ticket collectors had to be sent down to protect the railway's revenue. Some figures are given later. From the 1950s mass car ownership and changing social behaviour reduced this once regular flow to a mere trickle, but ramblers bound to and from the many beautiful walks across the North Downs are still seen, as indeed they are at Dorking.

A more recent development has been the use of the station for unloading the Down mail traffic for Dorking Post Office into road vans in the evenings. This followed an accident at Dorking whilst mailbags were being moved across from the Down platform to the roadway on the Up side.

Nowadays Boxhill's only privilege is that it remains open at all. Outside the Monday to Friday peak periods, there is but one call each way every hour, often enough doing no business at all, especially in winter.

The Line That Never Was

Dorking might have had another station and a third railway. To trace the origins of this we need to go back to proposals advanced from 1884 onwards that Midhurst and Cranleigh should be given a more direct route to London by a line which would join the existing LBSCR between Leatherhead and Holmwood. So far as the Dorking area was concerned, it was no doubt considered that such a facility might encourage high class residential development, and thus First Class rail traffic, on the southern slopes of Leith Hill and the greensand ridges either side, where there were already some large new houses. As the LBSCR served both Midhurst and Cranleigh, its support for any such scheme was important. The first proposal was for a 24-mile line from near Holmwood station to Midhurst via Cranleigh but this evoked no response from the LBSCR. That Company was however attracted by the idea of a branch to Cranleigh passing below the southern slopes of Leith Hill and seems also to have been exercised about the possibility of the LSWR coming south from Leatherhead. Dorking's citizens had also been restive for some time about the LBSCR's monopoly of the direct London route and there was a feeling in the town that the LSWR would be more than welcome.

These pressures and possibilities caused the LBSCR in 1897 to draw up plans for a single line, leaving the railway between Leatherhead and Dorking just south of Box Hill station, then passing north and west of the centre of Dorking before running south to Holmwood, where it would join a second new line from Holmwood station to Cranleigh via Ewhurst. A bill was prepared for the 1897-8 session of parliament.

In Dorking, the proposed railway was to cross Bradley Lane and Lord Ashcombe's Bradley Farm, demolishing the two pairs of cottages and gardens adjacent to the main line before passing through Mr. Appleby's Nursery (Boxhill Nursery) and the tennis ground. It would then go through the SER embankment, removing two houses opposite Pippbrook Mill before crossing the present Meadowbank recreation ground. At Archway Place five cottages would disappear. Traversing Station Road on arches at Washway Bridge, the line would then slice through the Drill Hall, crossing the Westcott Road on an arch. Part of the Vicarage garden on the West side of the stables would be required, also much of Sondes Place Farm. After crossing over Hampstead Lane on an arched bridge, the Nower was to be penetrated by a 200-yard tunnel. Beyond, Robert Barclay's land would be traversed. Further south the line was planned to run along the back of the *Norfolk Arms* at Mid-Holmwood, pass west of South Holmwood church and finally join the proposed Cranleigh line on the southwest side of Holmwood station. There can be little doubt that this railway was mainly intended to pre-empt any incursion of the LSWR into the Dorking area.

This was enough to arouse the opposition of the Dorkinians, who wanted a competing railway, not more of the same. They envied Leatherhead, already benefiting from competition, with relatively cheaper fares based on the shorter LSWR route to London[16]. Nor did they relish the disturbance to property involved, though this was fairly light and would be amply compensated. On the other hand there was some support for a Holmwood to Cranleigh line. These opinions were confirmed at a meeting held under the auspices of the Urban District Council in the Oddfellows' Hall on 8 January 1899. One speaker also expressed fears that the new line would bring day trippers 'with broken bottles, meat tins and sandwich papers after their manner' to Holmwood Common, which together with Redlands Wood, would become 'like Ashtead Common'. With one dissentient, the meeting passed a motion objecting to the Dorking-Holmwood loop, approving the Holmwood-Cranleigh line as desirable and requesting the Council to approach the LSWR regarding an extension to Dorking.

Lord Ashcombe of Denbies and A. H. Brown M.P., the then owner of Broome Hall, were also in influential opposition. Faced with this show of resistance, and perhaps now satisfied the LSWR had no intention of building a line into the Dorking area, the LBSCR deleted the scheme from its 1898 bill, returning to parliament the following year with just the Holmwood-Cranleigh proposal. This gesture removed the Dorking Council and Lord Ashcombe from opposition but brought other opposing landowners into the fight, as well as Surrey County Council, which did not like some aspects of the alignment proposed. The scheme failed in parliament in 1900, coming alive again as the Holmwood, Cranleigh, Midhurst and Havant Railway in 1905. Put forward as a more direct route from London to Portsmouth, this seems to have envisaged express working and perhaps Government support on strategic grounds, although its engineer was none other than the famous light railway king, Holman F. Stephens. However the LBSCR was not interested in working it, nor did any Government backing of substance emerge and the scheme died on the vine. Nothing more was heard of railways along the north western edge of The Weald.

It is amusing, if idle, to speculate on what might have happened had the west Dorking loop been built, as it surely would have been had the LSWR showed any real interest in coming south from Leatherhead. There is little doubt it would have given Dorking another station on the west side of the town, perhaps on the Westcott road, or that it would have encouraged the middle class residential development already evident in and around Westcott village. It is possible that a second station might have been built at Mid Holmwood, which was also showing signs of growth by the 1910s. Most trains would have terminated at Leatherhead or Epsom and it seems unlikely that through the day there would have been more than one an hour. After electrification of the main line, nothing would have run through to London. The limited commuter housing development in Dorking between the wars does not suggest that such an additional railway would have generated any substantial housing growth along its route but there might have been some lucrative First Class traffic for a while. If built, the line would not have survived the Beeching cuts of the early 1960s and might well have succumbed earlier. Its right of way would certainly have offered a fine alternative route for the A24 by pass in the late twenties, an alignment far more acceptable to the town than the shameful desecration of The Deepdene that was imposed in 1931.

Deepdene's Railway Era

Since it had a railway association, some reference must now be made to The Deepdene itself[17], that famous Dorking mansion and estate now no more. In June 1939, with the threat of a major European war increasing by the day, the SR bought the house, which in the 1920s had been converted to a country hotel. For the house and gardens the owner, L. R. Peters, received £21,200, a bill partly met by the Government since it was categorised as air raid precautions expenditure. The mansion and its outbuildings were then hurriedly converted to railway offices and operations rooms, to serve as the company's wartime headquarters, replacing the offices at Waterloo station which it seemed might well be wiped out in the early mass air attacks expected by the Government. Many staff were moved to Dorking at the beginning of September 1939, comprising the offices of the General Manager, Traffic Manager (including Superintendent of Operation and Locomotive Running Superintendent), Chief Engineer, Joint Accountant and Cashier. Staff servicing the Superannuation Fund and Savings Bank occupied the stable block north east of the mansion whilst those of the Audit Accountant's office at London Bridge station were accommodated in hutment offices on the east side of Dorking North station. Emergency ticket printing works were set up close by these huts.

Within three months of the outbreak of war, the strain of working from Deepdene during a period when there had been no attack of any kind on London proved too much. The Waterloo headquarters offices were reopened and some railway officers and staff returned there for the rest of the war, remaining despite air attacks. Nevertheless Deepdene was to play an important part in the railway's war. The general manager, Sir Eustace Missenden, took a house on the Deepdene Park Estate, dividing his time between Deepdene and Waterloo, whilst the Chief Engineer and the Traffic Manager were stationed at The Deepdene throughout the war. In old caves dug deeply into the greensand near the house, a telephone exchange and operations room were installed in case of air attacks or artillery bombardment by an invading force. Radio links were established with vital points on the SR system and motor cycle despatch riders were always on call.

Reference has already been made to the important part played by the railway in the evacuation of the Allied Forces from northern France in 1940, an operation controlled in large part from Deepdene. The Dorking headquarters was also involved in the movement of military freight and from 1944 played a major role in organising and monitoring the supply of the liberation forces in Western Europe, much of which was carried over the SR and through the railway-owned port of Southampton.

A special train ran daily from London Bridge to Dorking North via West Croydon for the benefit of Deepdene staff who had not moved into Dorking. Eventually this train appeared in the public timetable and it continued to run until the last railway staff left Deepdene in 1966. A bus was also provided to carry the less able-bodied up the hill from the station.

The dining room built at Deepdene by Thomas Hope in 1818 continued to serve as such during the railway's tenure. Its lavish decoration incorporated the golden-lily motif of Lilian, Dowager Duchess of Marlborough, who lived in the mansion from 1895 until 1909, although the effect was somewhat spoiled by the erection of large steam hoods over the serving area. The vast entrance hall added by Henry Hope in 1840, in which he had displayed statuary in arcades on two floors, still possessed its fine mosaic floor but the SR covered it completely with wood to protect it from wear. Typists occupied the billiard room, whilst the drawing room on the north-west front built by Thomas Hope in 1818 housed the Cash and Banking section and the 'new' drawing room of 1840 on the site of the former entrance hall was used by the Book-keeper and his staff.

On 22 October 1945 the Traffic Manager's staff returned to Waterloo, leaving the Chief Accountant, the Treasurer, the Bridges section of the Chief Engineer's Department and the Road Motor Engineer in The Deepdene and the Funds staff in the stable block. It was March 1966 before Dorking ceased to be a railway administrative centre. In that month the residue of staff at Deepdene and the audit clerks at the Dorking North station hutments moved to Southern House, Croydon.

Apart from first aid repairs, the railway era at Deepdene saw a general neglect of the fabric. Damage was done to the historic interior when partitions were erected in some rooms. After the war the lovely old building was alleged to be the greatest fire risk in Dorking and at the insistence of fire officers, an elaborate sprinkler system was installed in the late 1950s. The resulting intricate arrangement of exposed pipes protecting every room and corridor on each floor further injured the former splendour of the interior. These factors combined to ease the path of the property developers who purchased the mansion and its outbuildings, making it possible for them to obtain permission to demolish this Grade III listed building without too much difficulty. No doubt, it was with a great sigh of relief they ordered its demolition in 1969, since restoration and conversion would have been more costly than the garish white neo-brutalist office blocks which replaced it.

Before leaving the subject of World War 2, some other items of railway interest should be mentioned. It is surprising that the town and its strategically important railway installations suffered little serious damage from air attack. Whilst many strings of bombs were dropped in attempts to sever the railways where they crossed, most fell harmlessly in open countryside. Even when, on 24 May 1941, seven high explosive bombs did reach the railway just south of the bridge at the crossing of the two lines they only made craters at the lineside without damaging the permanent way.

Another wartime feature was the accommodation offered to Winston Churchill's Special Train, which found refuge for some time in the back road of the goods yard at Dorking North. Ready for immediate use when required, it was of course conveniently close to the control centre at The Deepdene.

It should be noted that this was not Churchill's only association with The Deepdene. In the 1890s and 1900s he had been a frequent visitor to the house when it was the residence of his uncle's widow, the Duchess of Marlborough. A passage in his book *My Early Life*, (1930) relates how once, when invited to attend a dinner at which the Prince of Wales (later Edward VII) was the principal guest, he unwisely delayed his departure from London, taking the 19.15 train down from London instead of the 18.00. About halfway, realising with horror that he was going to be late, he proceeded to change into evening dress between stations, much to the astonishment of the gentleman sharing his First Class compartment. He was whisked up the hill in a carriage from the house and on arrival found that the start of dinner had been delayed, since the superstitious Edward would not begin until Churchill made the number at table up to 14.

The Railways and The Town

There can be little doubt that Dorking's increasing popularity as a holiday and residential centre from the middle of the 19th century until World War 1 and its general prosperity in that period owed much to the excellent railway facilities. As mentioned earlier, the tourist potential had already been foreseen in Phelps' evidence to the RG&RR parliamentary committee and in its account of the cutting of the first sod at Betchworth, *The Illustrated London News* of 28 August 1847 picked up the same point, alluding to the picturesque nature of the eastern section:

. . . which will be new ground for many a tourist, though it is, perhaps, the most beautiful scenery of its class in England. Its landscapes present a rich succession of *bits* for the painter; in its picturesque uplands, woodland dells, verdant valleys, rocky hills, and undulating parks and heaths, all lying within the eye of the traveller along this new line.

Six years after the arrival of the SER, in 1855, the anonymous author of a guide book of the town noted:

In summer . . . many a man of business, who may be seen daily in the City, and who seems as though he were wedded to his counting house and his ledgers, is glad to daff the world aside, and spend his evenings at Dorking, for, thanks to the rail! the daily journey to and fro occupies no more time than the coach or omnibus drive to Hampstead or Highgate . . . Not only has the railroad improved the trade of the town, but it has in no small degree promoted the comfort of its inhabitants, who can now realize almost every advantage which a city affords, and be at the same time free denizens of the country, enjoying its peculiar charms and reaping all the benefits which it so freely offers[18].

Subsequent guide books to Surrey often mention the good rail access to the beautiful scenery around Dorking and many middle class holidaymakers were thus attracted to stay in the area. But whilst the railway was encouraging the more affluent Victorian Londoner to take a house or apartments in or around Dorking for his family for an extended period during the summer months, during which time he travelled up to work by train, at first its main impact was felt in the growth of day excursion traffic to the Box Hill and Dorking stations. This remained important until World War 2, not dying away completely until the early 1950s. Its demands led to the establishment of a new industry in the town, the manufacture and bottling of soft drinks by W. R. Butler & Sons Ltd. of Portland Road, as well as the opening of numerous tea rooms and refreshment houses. On the Cotmandene, holidaymakers were catered for by the construction around the 1880s of a tall block of short stay apartments. The second half of the 19th century also saw the opening of several small hotels in and around the town, supplementing the old-established inns.

Day trippers often made their presence felt. On Monday 24 August 1891 the United Society of Boilermakers and Iron Shipbuilders spent what was described, somewhat sadly, as 'their annual summer holiday' in the area. Marching with bands and banners from East India Dock to London Bridge station, they were conveyed in no less than five special trains to Dorking, arriving around midday. Nearly 5,000 men, women and children then marched from the station, still with their bands and banners, to the Cotmandene, where refreshments were served. When supplies ran out, the town was invaded and much beer was consumed. Eventually *The White Horse, The Red Lion* and *The Star & Garter* all closed their doors. The contemporary report in *The Surrey Advertiser*, from which this is drawn, reported scenes of drunkenness, much music, dancing and singing, but no arrests. One wonders whether the heavily outnumbered local police force simply barricaded themselves in their station. Imagine too the hard work put in by the railway staff in shepherding this inebriate mass of humanity safely on to their return trains.

A typical report, again from a local newspaper, shows that on Whit Monday 1895, the LBSCR carried about 4,000 excursionists into the area, about half this number alighting at Box Hill station. The SER was said to be equally busy and both lines worked special trains in addition to the normal timetable. Crowds of this size continued to arrive on the Easter, Whit and August Bank Holiday weekends right through to the 1930s. As late as August Monday 1938 there were 10,746 arrivals and departures at Box Hill station and 9,514 at Dorking North, a ten minute interval train service operating at the peak of the congestion.

The railways' contribution to the town's continuing prosperity continued after World War 1 despite an increasing challenge from motor transport. Indeed right up to the 1950s it was the railways which imported the bulk of the town's requirements for solid fuels and also all its building materials other than the locally-produced bricks and lime.

Railway-assisted residential development associated with the middle class London commuter was light and intermittent in the Dorking area before World War 1 and indeed hardly apparent until the last decade of the 19th century. This had much to do with the pace of the growth of the middle class but also to some extent reflected the unenterprising London train service offered by the SER and the LBSCR, which had agreements regulating competition and ensuring sharing of revenue. In 1912, William Shearburn, speaking at an Urban District Council meeting, remarked that it took over an hour to reach London by train, in some cases 80 or 90 minutes, whereas in 1865 the journey could be made in 65 minutes. He attributed this state of affairs to the lack of competition and suggested that the only hope was to get the LSWR to serve the town[19].

By the 1890s, A. H. Lyne & Co. had opened their house and estate agent's office in the approach to the LBSCR station and there was a modest daily flow of commuters. Estate agents were beginning to advertise in local guide books, concentrating on substantial properties. A residential handbook for 1912-13 was however only able to say 'Large and medium sized houses are obtainable as they become vacant, and a little building is going on'[20]. At first the commuters tended to be fairly wealthy members of the middle class, able to afford the longer journey time and the higher fare associated with living so far from London. Their large houses were at some distance from the station, around the outskirts of the town, at places like Westcott and their marginal income had to be sufficient to cover private transport to and from the station.

In the 1920s and 1930s, with a greatly improved train service following the 1925-29 electrification, residential growth accelerated. The town's population grew from 13,207 in 1921 to over 17,000 in mid 1938[21]. At this time, with the economic climate positively encouraging private housebuilding and the expansion of owner-occupation in south east England[22], Dorking houses came within the reach of a wider band of middle class pockets. Like most areas around London at this time, the town saw a boom in new house construction, especially in those parts within 10 to 15 minutes' walk of Dorking North station — around Ashcombe Road, either side of Deepdene Avenue, Deepdene Vale, and on the higher ground, the Deepdene Park and Park Copse developments[23]. Many of these houses were substantial detached properties standing in gardens of a quarter acre or more, the developers apparently considering that those able to consider the more expensive season ticket rates to Dorking would not be interested in the smaller type of house then being built in great numbers nearer to London. It is true that several small estates of more modest semi-detached houses of the suburban type did appear in the 1930s but almost all these were at a distance from the main station which suggests they were not primarily directed at commuters and were mainly bought by people working locally. Although Dorking has never been a dormitory town, and the majority of residents have always worked in the immediate area, the fact that there was a considerable growth in commuter traffic and housing in the between-wars period is confirmed by the increase in season ticket issues at Dorking North: these leapt from 669 in 1924 to 2,737 in 1932. (Ordinary ticket passengers in the same period increased from 207,505 to 455,585.)

A similar process took place in the same period on a much smaller scale close to Boxhill & Westhumble station, where the new electric services encouraged the building of scores of detached houses between 1934 and 1940 and again in the 1950s and 1960s, until all the available land within the Green Belt limits imposed after World War 2 was covered[24].

Although the spread of car ownership and dispersal of office work from the centre of London has reduced the flow of radial commuting since the mid 1960s, the daily movement at Dorking and Westhumble stations is still significant. At Dorking the extensive railway car parks are virtually filled up by 9.30 on Monday to Friday mornings. In 1982 the station handled a total of 649,000 passengers, over 55 per cent of them going to and from central London. At Boxhill & Westhumble the corresponding figures were 81,000 and 42 per cent. The Gatwick/Redhill and Guildford/Reading services carry a much lighter load but the trains on this line still bring many office and other workers and crowds of schoolchildren into the town every day, most of them through Dorking (Deepdene) station.

Dorking is indeed fortunate in its railway services; there are few country towns of its size which can still boast four stations and access by train not only to central and southwest surburban London and coastal resorts, but cross country facilities to most of the large provincial centres and a major airport. Although the frequency and speed of the London services has declined in the last 20 years and the direct coastal service has gone, Dorking effectively retains all the railway accommodation it has ever possessed. Today, from its Deepdene station, with but a single easy change of train at Reading, Guildford, Gatwick or Tonbridge, it is possible to reach Exeter and the West Country, Birmingham, Cardiff and South Wales, Oxford, Bristol, Manchester, Newcastle, Portsmouth and the Isle of Wight, Brighton and adjacent coastal resorts, Tunbridge Wells, Folkestone, Dover and many other destinations. By changing at Horsham, direct journeys can still be made to Portsmouth and the West Sussex towns.

It would be pleasant to think that Dorking could look forward to the 150th anniversary of its rail services in July 1999 without fear of any further deterioration in facilities but much will depend on the transport policies of future governments and above all the extent to which the

53

town's residents remain vigilant and make use of their railways. In this respect, the recent formation of a Dorking & District Rail Users' Association can be seen as an encouraging development in the right direction, deserving of more support.

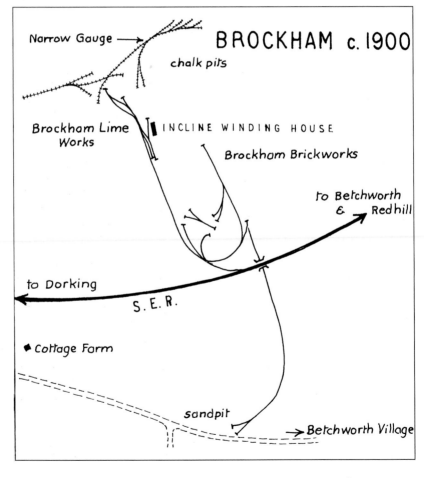

APPENDIX: THE INDUSTRIAL RAILWAYS

There were three separate industrial layouts in the Dorking Urban District.

The narrow gauge internal railways at the British Timber Works near the SER station (now Dorking West) have been mentioned in the main text. Little is known about them, but the layout appears on the 1914 and 1934 25 inch Ordnance Survey maps, somewhat extended towards the west end of the works in the latter. So far as is known, there were no locomotives, the wagons being moved by manpower or horses. No illustrations of the rolling stock or tracks have been found.

At North Holmwood, north of Inholms Lane, the Dorking Brick Company, later the Sussex and Dorking United Brick Co., and finally Redland Bricks, operated a 2ft gauge layout in their claypits and works, initially using horses. Four-wheeled battery electric locomotives were acquired in the early 1950s, one of which was converted in 1961 to automatic operation. Moving trains of tip wagons loaded with clay without a driver, this locomotive was brought to a stand on passing over a fixed ramp near the works. Ramps which could be raised or lowered according to the setting of the points were also fitted at junctions for the automatic haulage of these trains. At the works, loaded tip wagons of clay were pulled out of the pit up two separate inclines operated with ropes and a stationary winding engine. The brick works closed in 1981 and the site has since been covered with private housing.

The other industrial network was that serving the Brockham lime, hearthstone and brick works, sited approximately two miles east of Deepdene station. Chalk pits had been established here by the time the RG&RR was being built and application was made as early as 1848 to that company for a siding connection running north into the quarry. There was an internal narrow gauge system in what later also became a lime works (the 'Old Dorking Lime Works'), and by the 1890s a separate standard gauge layout serving the Brockham Brick Company's Works, which were adjacent to the north side of the SER and bounded on their west side by the standard gauge siding to the Lime Works, to which it was connected. At this time there was also a third line, of standard gauge, running south from the Brick Works under the SER to reach sandpits inside what is now the V formed by the A25 and the old Dorking to Betchworth road. The 1914 large scale Ordnance Survey map shows further extensions inside the Lime Works, chalk pits and hearthstone workings but by then the sand branch had been removed and most of the Brick Works layout had also disappeared, brickmaking having ceased some five years before. These changes followed the 1910 bankruptcy of the Brockham Brick Co. In the 1920s the lime works, then owned by The Brockham Lime and Hearthstone Company, were much run down, closing in 1934 (hearthstone extraction had ceased in

1925). Movement of wagons at the Brockham sites, both narrow and standard gauge, was undertaken by horses and men but the steeply-graded siding from the SER was worked by cable and a 16in. by 20in. steam haulage engine supplied by the Guildford firm of Filmer & Mason in 1874. By this means main line freight wagons brought coal up to the works and took out lime and hearthstone. By the early 1930s, the private siding, the only one in the area covered by this book, was the responsibility of the staff at Betchworth station but the key to the ground frame was kept at Dorking Town signal box, all traffic circulating from that direction. Wagons were exchanged immediately outside the gate leading into the workings, the key to this gate being kept by the owners. Following closure of Brockham Brick Company's activities, the private siding went out of use in 1935.

On 19 May 1962 the Brockham Lime Works and chalk pits were taken over by the Narrow Gauge Railway Society with the intention of establishing a working narrow gauge railway museum which would include items rescued from the adjacent Betchworth installation of the Dorking Greystone Lime Co. From 1966 this incipient museum was administered by the newly-formed Brockham Museum Association (later Trust). However Surrey County Council purchased the site in 1977 and serious problems arose over the granting of planning permission for a museum with full public access since the only road approach, via the Brockham level crossing of the Dorking-Redhill line, was narrow and unsurfaced. This led to the winding up of all activity on the Brockham site and amalgamation with the new (1979) Chalk Pits Museum at Amberley, Sussex, to which most of the exhibits were transferred.

Notes to the text

1. For an account of these earlier schemes, see Gray, Adrian, *The Railways of Mid-Sussex* (1975) and *The London & Brighton Line 1841-1977* (1977).

2. For a reproduction of all the minutes of the board of directors of the Reading, Guildford & Reigate Railway Company, from 1845 to 1852, together with an introduction by Edwin Course outlining the history of the railway and company, a reproduction of the Book of Reference for Dorking Parish, a description of the cutting of the first sod at Betchworth (from *The Illustrated London News* of 1847) and a select list of people associated with the railway, see Surrey Record Society Volume XXXIII, 1987.

3. Biddle, Gordon, *Victorian Stations*, David & Charles, 1973, p.39.

4. *The Railway Magazine*. April 1935, p.303.

5. Sellick, E. L., typescript in Dorking Museum (SCH/4 (i)).

6. *Dorking Advertiser*, 4 March 1966.

7. *The Sussex Agricultural Express (incorporating The Surrey Standard, Weald of Kent Mail & County Advertiser)*, 7 September 1850.

8. The Census Returns of 1851 show 2 stationmasters, 2 labourers, 9 porters, 2 firemen, 1 engine driver, 1 guard, 1 inspector and 2 watchmen living in Dorking Parish.

9. *The Reshaping of British Railways*, HMSO, 1963, Part 1: Report, p.112.

10. There may also have been an element of spite in Grissell's heavy reaction to the arrival of the LBSCR on his estate, not to mention a dash of hypocrisy. He had earlier been an active supporter (and provisional director) of a railway which would have cut through his property on much the same alignment. He was one of the promoters in 1855-7 of independent schemes proposing to link Dorking, Leatherhead, Epsom and Wimbledon on the LSWR, schemes designed to sell at a profit to either that company or the LBSCR, which were battling over access to Portsmouth. The first of these proposals, the Epsom and Leatherhead Railway, secured an act in July 1856, but the second (intended to absorb the first), the Wimbledon and Dorking, succeeded only in getting sanction for an Epsom-Wimbledon line, in July 1857. Both lines were subsequently taken over by the LSWR and the LBSCR and to some extent the intentions of their promoters were frustrated. (See Jackson, Alan A., 'Racing to Residential: The Wimbledon to Epsom Line', *Railway World*, July 1980, p.355.)

11. The essentials of the agreement between Grissell and the LBSCR are conveniently summarised in Turner, John Howard, *The London Brighton & South Coast Railway: II. Establishment & Growth*, (1978), pp.113-4.

12. Turner, op cit, p.115.

13. *The Illustrated London News*, 24 August 1867.

14. There was also a Craven 6ft. 'small' single tender engine no. 235 *Dorking*, built in November 1866; sold to the West Lancashire Railway in 1883, it continued to carry the now inappropriate name as that railway's no. 5 until scrapped in 1887. Apart from *Mickleham* (built 1874, scrapped 1904), the other 'D' tanks mentioned were long-lived. *Dorking* worked from 1884 until 1947, *Ranmore* from 1879 till 1948, *Denbies* from 1879 until 1936 and *Deepdene* from 1879 to 1926. The 'Terrier' *Boxhill* was built in 1880 and withdrawn from regular use in 1940.

15. Nelson, Victor H., 'Stroudley Reminiscences No. IV', *The Railway Magazine*, November 1932, p.336.

16. In the 1890s the annual season ticket rates between Dorking and London Bridge or Victoria were £22 Second Class and £27 First Class. These had been reduced from £24 and £30 in July 1890 in response to pressure from the Dorking Local Board and remained unchanged until World War 1. In contrast, at Leatherhead, just four miles nearer London, the Second Class season ticket holder paid only £16. In the 1920s the quarterly season ticket rate was £13.5s (£13.25) First Class, £8.17s.6d. (£8.875) Third Class (present Standard Class), available at all London SR termini and for intermediate use.

17. For an account of the history of The Deepdene up to modern times, see Mercer, Doris, *The Deepdene, Dorking: Rise and Decline Through Six Centuries*, reprinted from Vol. LXXI, 1977, Surrey Archaeological Collections for The Dorking & Leith Hill District Preservation Society, 1982.

18. Anon, *A Handbook of Dorking*, John Rowe, Dorking, 1855.

19. *Dorking & Leatherhead Advertiser* 31 August 1912.

20. Row, Prescott and Anderson, Arthur Henry (ed.), *Where to Live Round London (Southern Side)*, Fourth and Revised Edition, 1912-13, p.72.

21. These two figures are not strictly compatible; the Dorking area was expanded in 1928 to include North Holmwood and Pixham.

22. For the economic and financial background of the suburban housing boom, see Jackson, Alan A., *Semi-Detached London: Suburban Development, Life and Transport, 1900-39*, Allen & Unwin, 1973, chapters 6 and 11.

23. For an account of the building development in the Deepdene Park see Jackson, Alan A., *The Residential Development of Deepdene Park, Dorking, since 1920*, Dorking & Leith Hill District Preservation Society Local History Group, 1984.

24. For an account of the modern development of Westhumble see Shepperd, Ronald, *The Manor of Wistomble in the Parish of Mickleham*, Westhumble Association, 1982, pp.62-113.

Sources and Select Bibliography

Primary Sources

Bill and Parliamentary papers of the railways mentioned (Surrey Record Office and House of Lords Record Office)

Minutes of the Board of Directors, Reading, Guildford and Reigate Railway Company (Public Record Office: see also Course, below).

Agreement dated 19 March 1862 between Henry Thomas Hope (Deepdene) and the provisional directors of the Horsham, Dorking & Leatherhead Railway (copy in private hands).

Ordnance Survey Maps, Six and Twenty Five inches to the mile, various dates.

Bradshaw's Railway Guide, various dates.

Handbook of Stations, including Junctions, Sidings, Collieries, Works etc. on the Railways of the United Kingdom, showing the Station Accommodation, Crane Power, County, Company and Position, Railway Clearing House, 1904.

Table of Distances between Stations, Junctions &c on the London Brighton and South Coast Railway, January 1901, issued by the Accountant's Office, London Bridge, 24 December 1900.

Southern Railway Board and Committee Minutes, various dates (Public Record Office).

Southern Railway: General, Central-Eastern and Western Appendices to the Working Time Tables, Southern Railway, 26 March 1934 as amended to 16 April 1938.

Surrey County Council Public Transport Plans, 1983-4, 1984-5.

Printed Circular, *Proposed Holmwood, Cranleigh, Midhurst & Havant Railway, 1905*, issued by J. Buckwell & Co., solicitors, North Gate House, Brighton, 1905 (copy in private hands).

Oral reminiscences of Charles Wiscombe, Dorking, former LBSCR and SR employee, clerk and relief stationmaster, Dorking Town station, 1932-33.

Secondary Sources

Newspaper cuttings in Dorking & District Museum from *Dorking Advertiser, Surrey Advertiser, Surrey Mirror, Surrey Times*, 1880-1986.

Anon, *A Handbook of Dorking*, pub. by John Rowe, 1855.

Anon, *Electric Railway Traction Supplement, 'The Railway Gazette', Southern Railway Electrification Extension, Arundel, Littlehampton, Bognor Regis, Chichester and District*, 24 June 1938.

Anonymous item in *The Illustrated London News*, 24 August 1867.

Anonymous items in *The Railway Magazine:* — September 1925, p.229, April 1929, p.253, June 1934, p.406, March 1937, p.218, August 1938, p.102.

Acworth, W. M., *The Railways of England*, Fifth Edition, John Murray, 1900, p.369 (reference to collapse of Betchworth Tunnel).

Biddle, Gordon, *Victorian Stations*, David & Charles, 1973 (Dorking SER and LBSCR and Box Hill LBSCR stations).

Cooper, B. K., 'The Unknown Main Line', *Railway World*, August 1972, p.338.

Course, Edwin, *The Railways of Southern England: Secondary and Branch Lines*, Batsford, 1974, (Reading to Redhill line).

Course, Edwin, (editor), *Minutes of The Board of Directors of The Reading, Guildford & Reigate Railway Company*, Surrey Record Society Vol. XXXIII, 1987.

Darwin, Bernard, *War on The Line: The Story of The Southern Railway in War-Time*, Southern Railway, 1946.

Down, C. G., and Smith, D. H., *Brockham Museum Guide*, Second Edition, 1979.

E. G. B. (E. Gore-Brown?) 'Dorking and Its Three Stations', *Southern Railway Magazine* Vol. XI no. 123 (March 1933), p.94.

Evan, John (Simpson, E. J.), *Time Table for Victory*, The British Railways, nd (1946?).

Gairns, J. F., 'The Portsmouth Routes of The London Brighton and South Coast Railway', *The Railway Magazine*, September 1916, p.149.

Gilks, J. Spencer, 'The Reading, Guildford & Reigate', *Railway World*, February 1965, p.54.

Gould, David, *The South—Eastern & Chatham Railway in the 1914-18 War*, The Oakwood Press, 1981.

Gray, Adrian, *The Railways of Mid-Sussex*, The Oakwood Press, 1975.

Harrod, John, T. A., 'Up The Dorking' parts 1 and 8, *Southern Notebook* no. 84, Autumn 1984 p.123 and no. 90, Summer 1986, p.23.

Hart, H. W., 'The Holmwood, Cranleigh & Midhurst Railway', *Journal of the Railway & Canal Historical Society*, Vol. 8;5,6 and Vol. 9;1.

Harvey, Norman, 'Locomotive Variety Between Redhill and Reading', *The Railway World*, October 1961, p.327.

Hopwood, H. L., 'The Reading Branch of The South Eastern & Chatham Railway', *The Railway Magazine*, February 1918, p.73.

Kidner, R. W., *The Reading to Tonbridge Line*, Oakwood Press, 1974.

Mitchell, Vic, and Smith, Keith, *Epsom to Horsham*, Middleton Press, 1986 (this small book mainly comprises a selection of well-reproduced photographs and large scale plans of the area).

Moody, G. T., *Southern Electric: The History of the World's Largest Suburban Electrified System*, Ian Allan, Fourth Edition, 1968.

Neal, Andrew and Smith, David, *Industrial Railways of The South East*, Middleton Press, 1984.

Turner, John Howard, *The London, Brighton & South Coast Railway, II: Establishment and Growth, III: Completion and Maturity*, Batsford, 1978 and 1979.

Vallance, H. A., 'The Redhill-Reading Branch of The Southern Railway', *The Railway Magazine*, April 1937, p.235.

Vallance, H. A., 'To Brighton Through The Shoreham Gap', *The Railway Magazine*, February 1953, p.75.

'Voyageur' (Allen, Cecil J.), 'The Main Line Gradients of British Railways: XX Southern Railway Western Division Branches and Central Division Main Lines', and 'XXI — Southern Railway, Eastern Division', *The Railway Magazine*, August 1930, pp.144-5 and September 1930, pp.212-3.

Willox, W. A., and Lee, Charles E., 'Queen Victoria's Funeral Journey', *The Railway Magazine*, March 1940, pp.138-9.

INDEX

62